LIVING FELLOWSHIP

LIVING FELLOWSHIP

Helen Roseveare

HODDER & STOUGHTON
LONDON   SYDNEY   AUCKLAND

British Library Cataloguing in Publication Data

A catalogue record for this book is available from the British Library

ISBN 0-340-57073 3

Published by Hodder and Stoughton, a division of Hodder and Stoughton Ltd, Mill Road, Dunton Green, Sevenoaks, Kent TN13 2YA. Editorial Office: 47 Bedford Square, London WC1B 3DP.

Typeset by Phoenix Typesetting, Burley-in-Wharfedale, West Yorkshire.

Printed in Great Britain by Cox & Wyman Ltd, Reading.

Contents

Preface

It is many years since I began to pray and prepare my mind towards the writing of this book, the fourth in the series on 'The Four Pillars of WEC'. As a full-time serving missionary with WEC International, this project was suggested to me by the Mission leadership in 1976 and, over the intervening years, God has enabled the production of the first three books on Sacrifice, Faith, and Holiness. Only the fourth pillar, Fellowship, remained.

In 1986, as the manuscript began to take shape in my thoughts, I attended a missionary convention in Hamilton, Ontario, organised by Canadian Christian students as a means to challenge their peers to a lifetime commitment in the service of our Lord Jesus Christ.

Keith Price, a most godly and gracious Christian gentleman, gave four Bible studies at that convention. Not only did those studies speak deeply to my own heart, but they also confirmed, in wonderful detail, my own ponderings as to the true biblical meaning of the word 'fellowship'.

What follows is a filling-out of those studies as the Holy Spirit has underlined for me the double essentials of relationship and practice if we are to live in meaningful *koinonia* fellowship with God and His people in today's suffering world.

Helen Roseveare

WEC International,
Bulstrode, Gerrards Cross,
Bucks SL9 8SZ, England

Prologue

The Peace of the Fellowship of the Trinity

A hurricane spiralled its way across the valley to the east and up between the two hills which flanked the Nyankunde Medical Centre. To the south side of our thatched bungalow, the roof of Dr Ulrich's home was lifted and flung a hundred yards into the next valley. The torrential storm that followed burst on the doctor's unprotected family, huddled together in shock and fear in the roofless, ceilingless dining-room. Soaked through in a matter of seconds, they watched helplessly as lightning flashed across the skies, the destruction of all their household possessions.

To the north, on the other side of our home, first the Swiss nurses' home, and then the pilot's home, were similarly battered.

Centrally between the doctor's and the pilot's homes, a couple of hundred yards from each, our house stood undamaged. My friend and I were woken by the noise of the ferocious storm raging outside on all sides, initially unaware of what was occurring to others – at peace in the security of our undamaged home.

Peace – physical stillness – when all around was terrifying turmoil.

On Christmas Eve 1964, three British women missionaries with nine Belgian children made their way from the convent where they were being held prisoners, across the compound to the monastery where a carol service was to take place. Priests and male missionaries, also prisoners of the guerrilla regime, had made a rough manger-scene and persuaded the soldier-guards to allow the children to join them for a carol service. In the countryside all around the Catholic Mission compound, a vicious war was being waged between the Congolese National Army and the Simba guerrillas. During the five preceding and the two following months, over two hundred European and American missionaries (Catholic and Protestant) were brutally murdered and thousands of nationals tortured, mutilated and savagely butchered to death. In the midst of all this raging devastation, this small group of Christians worshipped God, singing carols around a simple manger scene.

Physical stillness, spiritual peace.

The word 'fellowship' is used today by an amazing variety of groups who often have very little in common between their members or their activities, frequently with little or no apparent peace. The word is used by political and socio-economic groups, as well as by Christians, to indicate sometimes nothing more than a gathering together for tea and biscuits! In fact, the Christian Church has allowed itself to be drawn in to the same loose usage of the word, with little regard to the true biblical meaning of the New Testament word, *koinonia*. Groups of people, with extraordinarily different opinions and convictions, have been drawn together by some means or other and are then said to be 'in fellowship' with each other, despite lack of harmony in their practices and even intolerance towards each other's beliefs.

In our many English translations of the Scriptures, the Greek word *koinonia* is variously translated as 'fellowship of sharing', 'participating', 'being partakers one of another', 'partnership', 'taking part in' something together, and also, from the same root, as 'having all things in common' – expressed also in words such as 'community' and 'communion'.

In his book *God's New Society* (IVP, 1979), John Stott

shows that it is only as we as individuals are saved by grace through faith that we become members of God's new society, the Church, the family of God's adopted children, and can therefore enjoy true fellowship one with another. Both Dr Martyn Lloyd-Jones, in *The Cross* (Banner of Truth, 1976), and John Stott in *The Cross of Christ* (IVP, 1976), have explained that this 'fellowship of believers' can only exist as each member is convinced of the centrality of the Cross in their own personal Christian lives. Biblical *koinonia* has no meaning if all the members do not have this one thing 'in common', that each one has individually put their trust in the death of Christ on the Cross for their redemption.

The Cross has to be the common attraction that draws members into the closely knit fellowship of the local church. However, this *koinonia* is not an exclusive club; it is not divisive and it is certainly not man-orientated. It is inclusive of all who believe; it is unitive for all who place their trust in Christ as Lord and Saviour; it is self-abnegating, as each member seeks to give for the good of others in the fellowship rather than to get from the group for one's own benefit. It is a fellowship based on love and loyalty, understanding and trust; a desire to see the other person's point of view rather than to gain one's own way; a willing-ness to be ignored, overlooked or misunderstood if this should be for the general good.

In his book *True Fellowship* (NavPress, 1986), Jerry Bridges reminds us that *koinonia* is not sitting around, drinking coffee together and talking about everything and anything in our daily lives. He says: 'True fellowship is not Christian social interaction . . . it is not an activity: it is a relationship.' He goes on to show very clearly that as we relate firstly to God Himself by the new birth and adoption into His family, so secondly can we relate to all other members of His family, that is, the Church. As we so relate, we shall want to share both our spiritual life and our material possessions. It is this two-way re-lationship and two-way sharing together that constitute, at least in part, *koinonia* in its truest biblical sense.

The doctrinal meaning of *koinonia*, as it is promised to all members of the visible Church of the Lord Jesus Christ here on earth, can only be rightly understood as we recognise the fellowship that exists between the three Persons of the Trinity.

These three Persons act together, most noticeably in creation and in the redemption of mankind, in perfect harmony. We can hear God saying in Genesis 1:26: 'Let us make man in our image,' and then read of each Person of the Trinity playing His part in that creative act:

> In the beginning God created the heavens and the earth . . . and the Spirit of God was hovering over the waters (Gen. 1:1–2).

> God . . . has spoken to us by his Son . . . through whom he made the universe (Heb. 1:2).

> In the beginning was the Word . . . and the Word was God . . . Through him all things were made (John 1:1–3).

They work in the same harmony in procuring the redemption of man.

God the Father preordained that His Son should be put to death 'by nailing him to the Cross' (Acts 2:23) and so He chose us in Christ 'before the creation of the world' (Eph. 1:4).

God the Son 'loved [us] and gave himself for [us]' (Gal. 2:20). Did He not say, of the Good Shepherd, 'I lay down my life . . . no-one takes it from me, but I lay it down of my own accord' (John 10:17–18)?

God the Spirit makes this redemption real in the heart of each believer. Not only are we to be 'born of the Spirit' (John 3:8) and so become 'new creations' in Christ (2 Cor. 5:17), but we are to know that we are saved; we are to understand what God has wrought for us. 'God has revealed [all this] to us by his Spirit' (1 Cor. 2:10).

This harmonious working of the Trinity brings peace into the heart of each believer. 'The Counsellor, the Holy Spirit, whom the Father will send in my name,' Christ said to His disciples, 'will teach you all things and will remind you of everything I have said to you. Peace I leave with you,' Christ continued, as though the very presence of the Holy Spirit would in itself bestow that very peace. 'My peace I give you' (John 14:26–7).

'Christ Jesus . . . is our peace,' Paul wrote to the Ephesians, as he explained how, by His death on the Cross, Christ had broken down the dividing wall of hostility that existed between us and God, and between us and others: 'His purpose was to create in himself one new man out of the two, thus making peace' (Eph. 2:13–15).

Furthermore, the three Persons of the Trinity not only work together in perfect fellowship, but also they claim equality, the One with each Other. The Son, our Lord Jesus Christ, claimed equality and unity with His Father, and the Father and the Son state they are equal to the Spirit: 'I and the Father are one,' Jesus explicitly stated (John 10:30).

' "My Father is always at his work to this very day, and I, too, am working." For this reason the Jews tried all the harder to kill him; not only was he breaking the Sabbath, but he was even calling God his own Father, making himself equal with God' (John 5:17–18).

Jesus then claimed that the Spirit proceeded from them. 'When the Counsellor comes, whom I will send to you from the Father, the Spirit of truth who goes out from the Father, he will testify about me' (John 15:26).

Jesus prayed that Christians would know this same unity among themselves as He and His Father and the Spirit enjoyed among themselves (John 17:21–3): '. . . that all of them may be one, Father, just as you are in me and I am in you. May they also be in us so that the world may believe that you have sent me. I have given them the glory that you gave me, that they may be one as we are one: I in them and you in me. May they be brought to complete unity . . . '

Such unity will indeed be the basis of true fellowship, and this in turn will bring about true peace.

So, firstly we are to have fellowship with God, our fellowship being with the Father and with His Son, Jesus Christ (1 John 1:3), and also with the Spirit (Phil. 2:1). In the following chapters, we shall seek to understand clearly that this fellowship flows out of a definite and personal relationship which manifests itself in certain practices.

However, that is only the first step to understanding the full meaning of biblical *koinonia*, for not only are we to enter into true fellowship with God, but this is also then to work out into fellowship with other members of the Body. John declares that we are to 'have fellowship with one another' (1 John 1:7–10). Here again, this fellowship has to flow out of a clearly understood relationship which will manifest itself in practical ways to the common good. Luke described this so clearly between believers in the early Church:

> Those who accepted [Peter's] message were baptised, and about three thousand were added to [the Church's] number that day. They devoted themselves to the apostles' teaching and to the fellowship, to the breaking of bread and to prayer. Everyone was filled with awe, and many wonders and miraculous signs were done by the apostles. All the believers were together and had everything in common. Selling their possessions and goods, they gave to anyone as he had need. Every day they continued to meet together in the temple courts. They broke bread in their homes and ate together with glad and sincere hearts, praising God and enjoying the favour of all the people (Acts 2:41–7).

Then thirdly, there is a yet deeper aspect to *koinonia*. Paul invites us to take part in 'the fellowship of sharing in his sufferings' (Phil. 3:10). If we are willing to be led by the Spirit into an understanding of this deep mystery, the threefold cord of *koinonia* will be complete.

So, as we move forward into the development of biblical fellowship, we will need to look in more detail, firstly at the upward stretch of fellowship between the individual and God Himself; secondly, we shall seek to understand the outstretched hand of fellowship between an individual Christian and his fellow-man; and lastly, we shall dare to enter into the mystery that is fellowship in the suffering of God for the world in which we live.

Each of these three areas of fellowship depends initially on a vital relationship between the parties involved, which will then manifest itself in certain practical activities. As we look at each of the three relationships, I shall use the allegory of a wheel: the relationship of the hub to the spokes, the relationship of the spokes to the surrounding rim, and the relationship of the hub to the rim, albeit via the spokes.

Then, as we turn from thinking of these relationships to realise how they can be worked out in the practicalities of our daily lives, I have used three specific symbols from the life of our Lord Jesus Christ – the yoke, the towel and the cup – to help us come to grips with all that is involved in vital *koinonia*. These three symbols have been thought of as forming the three sides of a triangle.

True fellowship is actually right relationships worked out in our lives in practical ways. Such relationships bring peace. This is the peace that the Lord Jesus promised us; it is the peace that He made available to us when He died on the Cross as our substitute; it is 'the peace of God that transcends all understanding' (Phil. 4:7).

Peace is the obvious and invariable fruit of biblical *koinonia* – fellowship with God, fellowship with our fellow-men, and fellowship in suffering 'for his name' – peace with God, peace with ourselves and peace with each other.

PART I

OUR FELLOWSHIP WITH GOD

1

Our Relationship with God: the Hub

How succinct is the writing of the Holy Spirit!
'Complete in him,' (Col. 2:10, AV).

In three short words He sums up the basis of all true fellowship – that is, the relationship of being united to Him.

And Who is the 'him'? None other than God Almighty, revealed to us in all His fulness by the Lord Jesus Christ, the Word made flesh and dwelling among us. Paul wrote, 'For in him [Christ] dwelleth all the fulness of the Godhead bodily. And ye are complete in him . . . ' (Col. 2:9–10, AV).

And if we are 'complete in him', it does not take a vast training in logic to deduce that we are *in*complete *out of* Him. How many of us have known the feeling of incompleteness at one time or another – maybe a sense of failure, or of insecurity, or of sheer inadequacy for the task that lies ahead of us?

As ambassadors for Christ, commissioned by God to preach the Word of Reconciliation, how many of us have known the acute sense of failure when, having preached clearly and with deep conviction of the power of the indwelling Holy Spirit of God to keep us from sin and to give us victory in both our private and public lives, we have failed Him miserably, perhaps by an outburst of uncontrolled anger over some petty, almost insignificant, event?

Have we not all known moments of insecurity, despite

having professed our total faith in God to provide for our every need at every level? When at the end there is no money available to meet an urgent bill (yet we're certain that the acquisition was God-prompted in the fulfilment of His purpose), have we not then known a moment of bewilderment, fear, or doubt, or questioned our guidance?

As a missionary in a foreign land, I have known inadequacy and frustration. Imagine having the diagnosis of a patient's illness, but being unable to treat him because of not having the needed drug in the pharmacy, and having no means to acquire it within the next six months! How frustrating to be ready to put the roof on a new building, perhaps a ward for the hospital, only to find that the nails that were eventually delivered last week were the wrong kind for corrugated sheeting! How frustrating to have made a 200-mile journey over the mountain range of Central Africa to pick up much needed supplies, only to find they were impounded by Customs and could not be released without a particular sheet of paper that might take up to a year to obtain!

Doubtless all of us could add endless examples, from whatever our particular walk of life – the frustration of the housewife who has cooked the evening meal and the family do not return on time and the soufflé is spoiled; the frustration of a school teacher who has prepared everything for the scheduled inspection, only to be told at the last minute that the government officials are not coming for another month; the frustration of a busy executive who has flown across the Atlantic to an important conference, only to find that the telegram announcing its cancellation had arrived one hour after he had left his homeland!

In each instance, and in numerous other similar instances, there is nothing wrong with the sense of frustration, but when one reacts to it with impatience, annoyance, or by blaming the other party, or in some such manner demonstrating a real lack of peace and of acceptance of the difficulties of working in an imperfect world, or in a developing country, then one realises one's 'incompleteness'. Had I been 'complete in him', I would have maintained His serenity and used the situation to prove His all-sufficient grace.

Some of us feel incomplete because we have never yet come to the Lord Jesus Christ on His terms. I make no apology for so-called 'old-fashioned' vocabulary when I say that the only acceptable way to come to Christ is as a sinner who needs saving, and who knows he/she cannot save him/herself.

From 1939 to 1944, during World War II, as a boarding schoolgirl in North Wales I had occasion to travel across the city of London six times every year, on my way to and from my home in Kent; and I had seen the bombing, the devastation, the horrific scenes after the crashing to earth of the dreaded doodle-bugs, causing destruction and death on all sides. And I had concluded that, if there were a God, He was irrelevant. He could not cope. He could not stop this slaughter, this futile cruelty of man against man, this barbarous savagery that a hunger for power caused as one nation sought to take over another.

Yet, at the same time as my mind reasoned 'There is no God,' my heart was crying out in hunger to know that very God whose existence I denied. I needed an all-powerful God, on whom I could depend and from whom I could seek answers to the many problems and questions that crowded in on all sides as the war progressed.

In 1944 I went up to university. It was still wartime. I was hungry for friendship, lonely and strangely frightened in the brave new world of university life. All the security of the rigid props of a girls' boarding school had suddenly been taken away and there was nothing to replace them. Along with many others, I was questioning everything, and there seemed to be no one to give any answers. In fact, there seemed to be no answers. What was the point of living? What was the purpose of it all?

I kept up a bluff exterior, probably appearing to others as self-reliant, competent, self-assured and able to cope with all I met. But inside I was chewed up with shyness, inexplicable fears and an almost desperate sense of inadequacy. How I longed to escape from it all! Only pride (plus, perhaps, fear of my father's reaction) kept me from running away – or even from ending the seeming uselessness of living, at all.

At that point, a Christian second-year student invited me to accompany her the following Sunday evening to a special Freshers' Sermon to be given in a large church in the centre of town. I accepted – not with any desire to go to church, but out of courtesy, plus probably the sheer need to be with someone instead of endlessly being on my own. After the evening meal we cycled down-town and, like hundreds of others, padlocked our bicycles to the iron railings surrounding the church. Holy Trinity was packed with students, and filled with an indefinable sense of belonging and of quiet expectancy – and I felt an outsider. The text, 'For there is one God and one mediator between God and men, the man Christ Jesus' (1 Tim. 2:5), is all I remember of the service. I was too self-conscious to be able to concentrate on the preacher or his message.

At the close, we left the building and walked across to collect our bicycles. And I burst out laughing! The girl who had taken me swung round to see what had amused me, and quick as lightning she said, 'Helen, that is just what your life is like!'

Next to my old, second-hand, sit-up-and-beg Raleigh bicycle, with its chipped black paint, there *had* been a beautiful new, modern, brightly coloured, well-equipped bicycle, padlocked to the railings with a very expensive padlock. It had gone. A thief had come during the service. Unable to break through the expensive padlock, he had taken out the hub of the front wheel and gone with the beautiful bicycle, leaving only the tangled mass of spokes in the abandoned rim – still duly padlocked to the railings with its obviously expensive padlock. It did look ludicrous – though I doubt if the owner thought so when he came to collect it!

I did not register my companion's remark at the time, nor would I then have been able to understand what she meant – but in the ensuing months, it kept coming back to me, even in my sleep. The sight of that tragic wheel, with no hub and no bicycle, and the words: 'That is just what your life is like!'

Yet, in a strange way, it was true, heart-achingly true. My life was in a mess, and the mess grew daily more tangled. I had no real friends, though many offered me friendship, but I hadn't learnt to give of myself or to trust others. I was scared. Lectures presented material beyond my understanding, and I didn't know to whom to turn for help. Tutorials became a nightmare, with the dread of being asked questions that I could not answer, and therefore of being made to look a fool in front of others. I was not relating to anyone else: I was alone, and I didn't know where I was going. The world seemed very large and very menacing. There seemed no meaning or purpose. Why live? Why not finish it off?

And I kept seeing visions of those tangled spokes . . . and no hub . . . and the uselessness of a bicycle without a hub in the centre of the wheel.

What was missing from my life? Why could I barely function as a rational human being? Who could help me to find the answers to life's questions that were becoming so poignantly pressing?

Members of our College Christian Union were only waiting for the right moment to move in and help. They offered me friendship and companionship. Their kindness lasted and did not evaporate, as I had feared it would. They didn't push themselves at me but always seemed to be around when I needed help. I began going to their meetings, listening in to the Bible studies and the prayer meetings, amazed at the quiet happiness and sense of security that pervaded the group.

So I began to learn of the great Creator God, who loved and cared and understood; who sent His only Son to be

born into this world as the Babe at Bethlehem in order
that He might die in the place of sinful men. Born to
die! That was a fantastic thought, yet it all made sense
as they showed me these truths from the Scriptures.
God cared so much, even for me, that He was willing
to die instead of me – amazing grace!

At last this lovely Saviour won my heart, and I asked
His forgiveness for all my pride and stubbornness,
resistance and rebellion over the past years. His peace
flooded my whole being, and suddenly I understood
that comment, as we had looked at a bicycle wheel
without a hub: 'That's just what your life is like!' The
Lord Jesus Christ, by the ministry of the Holy Spirit,
came into my life, as a Hub into a tangled wheel . . . and
He sorted me out, and made sense and order to reign
where before there had only been fear and disorder.

Some twenty-five years later, very early one morning,
I met an African at the roadside in Uganda. After the
usual courtesies, he asked me (in Swahili) if I was 'a
sent-one'. Taken aback by the bluntness of his question,
I thought quickly that that was the real meaning of the
word 'missionary', so I replied that I was a sent-one, yes,
but my usefulness as such depended on the Person by
whom I was sent and the mission for which I was sent.

'Are you a sent-one by a great God to tell me about
something called Jesus?' the man asked.

He was an illiterate herdsman, looking after his
family's cattle. Awed at his question, and with a keen
sense of privilege and of destiny, I sat beside him at the
roadside in the early morning sunshine, and with the
help of a book of coloured pages I explained to him
the basic truths of the Gospel.

Yes, there is a great God, who created all the wonderful and beautiful world around us, and also men and
women in that world, that we might love, serve and
worship Him. But over the years we men have chosen
to love, serve and worship ourselves, rather than God.
And what a mess we have made of God's world as a

result. The great God has written a book (holding my Bible in my hand) in which He calls that mess *sin*. And He, the Creator, has judged that the wages of sin, our just deserts that each one of us has earned by our own free choice, is death, that is to say, spiritual death – to live eternally separated from Him who would have been our friend and counsellor.

Turning from the black page, that represented our sin, to the red page, I shared with my herdsman friend the wonderful story of the birth of the Baby at Bethlehem, when the great God became one of us men. He was born as a Man in order that He might die for us – to take our wages – so that we might live. Using local African illustrations to help him enter into the wonder of that amazing story, I watched, fascinated, as light slowly dawned in his eyes, as he grasped at least the basic fact that the Creator so loved His creatures, despite all we had done to forfeit that love, that He was willing to die for us.

Turning from the red page, that represented the shed blood of our Saviour, to the following white page, I sought to explain our need to confess our sins individually and to ask Him for His forgiveness, that our hearts might be cleansed and made 'white as snow'. I was praying earnestly that God would give him understanding that that death on the Cross of Calvary two thousand years ago was sufficient to pay for all his (and my) personal guilt. It was awesome to watch that humble man open up to the Saviour, and to realise that he had passed from death to life, becoming a child of God and receiving the gift of eternal life.

We sat and talked together for nearly two hours. Then I got up to go back to the car and continue my journey homewards. As we approached the road another African, on his way to the local market, was cycling towards us with a huge head of bananas strapped to his carrier. As we watched him he suddenly swerved, and we saw the hub of the front wheel disengaging itself! He crashed to the ground, bananas in every direction.

We rushed to his rescue as he picked himself up and looked ruefully at his broken bicycle.

It was all I could do not to laugh out loud! But together we did what we could to help put the bicycle back together again, to gather up the scattered bananas, and to wave the lad off on his journey. Turning to my herdsman friend, I told him of my encounter, all those years before, with a bicycle wheel without a hub, and of how that had been used by God to bring me to a knowledge of my need of a Saviour. We laughed together as we recollected the look on the lad's face as he crashed to the ground, before we helped him on his way, and as we realised how totally helpless a bicycle wheel is without a hub. Yes, indeed, a human life without Christ as its Saviour is like a wheel without a hub: incomplete and therefore useless and quite unable to function in the way for which it was created.

With the hub in place, the wheel is complete and able to function correctly. With Christ in our heart as our Lord and Saviour, we are complete, 'complete in Him', and so able to function as God intended we should.

A few years ago, seeking to offer friendship to a lonely, sad lady at a Christian holiday centre, I became increasingly conscious of her total lack of assurance of salvation. To my question: 'Dear, if you were to die shortly, do you know that you would go to heaven?' her evasive reply was a hesitant: 'I hope so.' To a more blunt question, 'Do you know that your sins have been forgiven?' she only queried: 'Can one ever be sure of that?'

So I had the joy and privilege of sharing with her the story of my herdsman friend, using the same 'wordless book' to explain the way of salvation, but now employing illustrations from our western culture rather than African ones, to make it clear to her.

There was an obvious growing desire to believe what I told her, but yet there was also a reluctant hesitancy.

'That is all right for an African,' she started to say, and then faltered into silence. I understood what was troubling her, though she was afraid to put it into words, not wanting to appear offensive. That I had gone as a missionary to what used to be popularly called 'Black Africa' to tell a 'native' that he needed to be saved, was acceptable – but that she, a well-educated white lady, should need to come to God by the same route – that was revolutionary to her!

'Let me share another experience with you,' I said gently. 'Not long ago, I was coming home from shopping in our local city. I bought a railway ticket and went down to wait for my train on the appropriate platform. It was raining and I put up my umbrella. Another lady followed me down the slope, but she had no umbrella. I invited her to share mine and, as we stood together, an absolute cloud-burst occurred. I knew she would not go away from me in a hurry, and prayed quickly for some way to start a conversation with her.

'On the other side of the tracks there was a large poster for a brand of cigarettes. "That makes me annoyed," I said, pointing across the line. She looked at me, possibly a little belligerently. "Well," I said, "that makes young folk want to smoke; smoking causes lung cancer; lung cancer causes death."

'To my consternation, she broke down and began to cry. A train drew in to the platform. I assisted her in, sat beside her and asked if I could help her in any way.

' "I have just come from the hospital," she said, "where I had gone for a medical check-up, and they tell me that I am dying of lung cancer because I have smoked all my life."

'I felt awed, realising that only God could have caused me to say just what I had said at that particular moment to that particular lady. Praying quickly for help, I pulled out a pocket Bible, opened it and took out a small copy of the same wordless book. As the train made its way towards our destination, as simply as I could I went through the same explanation of the Way of Salvation with that dear lady as I had done with the African herdsman. There is only one way to come to

God, whether we are white-skinned or dark-skinned, whether we are highly educated or less so, whether we are rich in this world's goods or poor.'

That lonely guest at the holiday centre began to realise that God's salvation was for all, because all have sinned and come short of His glory. Slowly she opened her heart to accept His offer of forgiveness. Gradually she entered into a full assurance that her sins were forgiven because of Christ's death on the Cross, and that she would go at last to heaven, saved by His precious blood. She came to know without a shadow of doubt that by His grace, she was 'complete in Him'.

But, of course, most of my readers will know all this. Most will have invited the Lord Jesus Christ into their lives to be their own personal Saviour, possibly years ago. And yet we all know that there can still be, from time to time, a sense of incompleteness, of failure, of inadequacy. What has gone wrong? God did not mean us to be incomplete.

Is it, perhaps, that we have not kept close enough to our Redeemer? We have not applied spiritual oil to the human ball-bearings that make the activity of the hub easy and smooth running. The hub is in place, the spokes are correctly aligned, but the whole has been taken for granted and sadly neglected.

On some occasions when I first lived in Africa, I might send for an African and ask him to go perhaps to the nearest town to collect the monthly mail; or perhaps to another village to take medicines to someone in need; or to my Missionary Leader to take the hospital's quarterly report. Immediately he would reply with a request: 'May I please borrow one of your bicycles? And Doctor, please, not the cr-cr one, but the swsh-swsh one!' I knew what he meant!

One of the cycles in my shed had not been well-looked-after and the ball-bearings in the hubs were rusted. It was hard to ride – all right on the level and downhill, but impossible uphill. And you heard it when it was coming – cr-cr: cr-cr. The other cycle, considerably newer, was in far better condition, constantly cared for and oiled. It ran smoothly and could be ridden uphill as well as on the level. And it didn't really make any noise, just a gentle swsh-swsh as you rode along.

How easy for us to become 'cr-cr' Christians! I'm sure you know the type of person I am referring to, always with a grumble or complaint, always seeing the cloud and not its silver lining. And I'm afraid, during my first four years on the mission field, I certainly became a 'cr-cr' Christian.

I went to Africa in 1953 as a young, enthusiastic missionary, full of good intentions and high resolves. I truly wanted to be the best I could be, to please my Master and to serve the African Church in His Name. The vision seemed clear, my determination could not be faulted. But in the ensuing years, things did not work out as I had planned.

I was the only missionary doctor in an area of some 240,000 square kilometres, where roughly half a million people lived in thousands of tiny scattered villages. Roads were rudimentary, often only beaten-earth tracks. Transport was practically non-existent, apart from the occasional missionary's car or colonial planter's truck. Sickness was rampant, and death took its toll of infants, youths, young men and women. There were hardly any grey-headed senior citizens anywhere in our district.

Missionary nurses and paramedical helpers had done their best to provide a basic care programme in the centres where we worked. Some had made Trojan efforts to train national nursing-aids to care for their own people. But the sum total was woefully inadequate for the vast problem that faced us.

I travelled extensively in my first six months out there, and saw more and more of the appalling need: mothers dying in childbirth, men crippled with wrongly set broken legs, little children with bloated stomachs and spindle legs, with anaemias, malnutrition, intestinal worms and infections – pain, pain, pain. Everywhere I went, this crushing realisation of a people in pain, a people in need of help – a people looking to me to alleviate that pain, and to provide the help they needed.

I was overwhelmed, frightened, crushed. How could I ever come up to their expectations? How could I meet 1 per cent of their need, let alone 100 per cent? My inadequacy screamed at me. The vastness of the problem mocked me and crushed me. I almost turned-tail and ran. But . . . God stepped in.

One night, as I slept He gave me a vision. I awoke in the morning, awed and fearful. It was so clear, so complete. I was to create a small central hospital, develop a training school for African paramedical workers, and then work outwards from the centre to cover the whole vast region with a network of clinics. As the young men became qualified and able to carry responsibility, we were to open these clinics in ever-widening circles round the initial centre: rural hospitals with maternity care and child-welfare clinics, tuberculosis and leprosy care centres. Each would be linked to the Centre by regular visits from the doctor-in-charge, carrying medical supplies and equipment – at first by truck, later by aeroplane.

The scheme was dauntingly simple and yet it appeared to me at that time as outlandishly unattainable. Who would build? Who would pay? Who would teach? Questions poured into my mind, but nothing could dim the clarity of that first vision. I knew, instinctively, it was of God. I also felt I knew, equally instinctively, that the probable answer to most of my basic questions was myself! That at first scared me, but then challenged me. And I set out to turn the vision into reality.

I was prepared to put everything into the task. I gathered a team of national workers around me. Being almost a workaholic, I couldn't see why everyone else shouldn't be the same. I could work eighteen hours a day; why shouldn't the team? I could do without a midday meal; why shouldn't they? And I drove rough-shod over everyone else's plans and rights to self-expression. I had a vision, obviously given by God, so everyone ought to pull their weight to help me put it into operation – or so I reasoned.

It is not hard to understand why I became somewhat unpopular with Africans and fellow-missionaries. I was considered practically 'impossible to live with'. Other missionaries were willing to be posted anywhere, to work at anything, with anyone, so long as they were not asked to come to Nebobongo and share with me. And only I was blind to the problem.

Lots of silly little things could be quoted to illustrate the point. Let me share just one.

'I' was in charge at Nebobongo, the small village that had grown up around the hospital and medical work of our Mission. All members of the village met together in the church every morning at 6.30 a.m. for Bible study before going to our various jobs for the day. My African colleague, Pastor Agoya, was responsible for beating the drum at 6.20 a.m., so that everyone would be there in time for me to start Bible study with them punctually at 6.30 a.m. Being humans, from time to time we forgot to wind our watches – those were the days before the arrival of quartz time-keeping devices! Not having radios, we could not tune in to hear the BBC 'pips' at 6.0 a.m. and so put our watches right for the coming day. So what to do?

No problem! We had a particular bird who started to sing at 5.25 a.m. each morning, and when we heard 'the bird', we put our watches right! Very easy – except for one difficulty. We could easily hear different birds! One morning the pastor woke late and, hearing the bird, put his watch to 5.25 a.m., whereas mine already said 5.40 a.m. The drum was quarter of an hour late (by my watch) . . . and I was annoyed! It would spoil my whole day. Everything would be late and I just wouldn't be able to fit in all my programme. Another day the pastor woke before me and heard his bird and put his watch right to 5.25 a.m. I woke late that day, and equally put my watch 'right' when I heard my bird, but the pastor's watch by then said 5.40 a.m. So the drum, according to my reckoning, went quarter of an hour early that day – and I was irritated! I wasn't ready. I hadn't finished my preparation for the Bible study.

Why was I upset? Because 'I' was in charge, and so had the right to say which was the right bird!

Pathetic? Immature? You couldn't possibly have been so childish? I agree, but that is how it was, because 'I' was in charge, and I hadn't yet learned to hand over all the controls to my Master. Oh, yes, the Lord Jesus Christ had entered my life to be the Hub of my wheel, but the 'oil' was sadly lacking, and I was fast becoming a 'cr-cr' Christian. The close relationship between myself and my Lord was not being maintained. In no way was this His fault: it was entirely mine. I was allowing myself to become too busy, too involved working for God to be careful enough to take time to listen to what He wanted to say to me. And things were fast slipping from bad to worse.

Doing a morning ward-round among the women and children, I was angered on one occasion because something I had asked to be done the day before had been overlooked. My anger was an expression of my frustration; I was not learning to adapt my western medical practice to my African cultural setting. Why could they not remember? Why hadn't they understood how important it was for the patient's well-being? I might as well have said: 'With eighteen months' training from me, following their four or five years of primary education, why weren't they all qualified doctors?'

I had spoken hastily and harshly, publicly rebuking the student concerned for his negligence. A stony silence settled over the ward. Thirty-two village women looked at me, the missionary doctor who had come to live amongst them in order to tell them of the Lord. I had lost my temper over some small thing that so far as they were concerned was quite trivial.

I left the ward with John Mangadima, my African medical assistant. Only two years previously he had been my student. Now 'qualified' from my small 'medical' school, he had completed two years' training at Bible School before coming back to help me. We crossed the compound together to go to the men's ward. Quietly, almost apologetically, he spoke to me. 'Doctor,' he said, 'I don't think Jesus would have spoken like that.'

How right he was, but how humiliating to be told it by my own ex-student! We went back to the women's ward where I apologised for what had taken place. Inside me, questions tumbled over each other. Why did I fail so often? Why was I so unpopular that fellow-missionaries did not want to be appointed to work at Nebobongo? Why was I always so tired? I knew I carried a heavy workload and never-ending responsibility for lives, with no medical colleague with whom to share, but these were somehow just excuses and did not satisfy me. I knew perfectly well they were inadequate reasons. God could give one victory: He had promised all-sufficient grace for each day's needs. He was there, willing to dwell within me and live out His perfect and holy life through me, but somehow I had lost touch.

Our senior pastor, Ndugu, was watching and praying. He saw my spiritual need and had rightly diagnosed the root cause of my problem. He came for me one Friday afternoon, having made all necessary arrangements for me to have a week's break out at his village. Rucksack on my back, I cycled out the twenty-five kilometres behind him. His wife had prepared a room for me in their home. Broken and feeling a complete failure, I settled down for a weekend alone with God, to seek to get right with Him and to make a fresh start. But by Sunday evening I had got nowhere. Heaven seemed like brass. I could find no answer in the Bible. God seemed remote, out of reach.

Going to the front door, I looked out and saw my pastor and his wife sitting by the embers of the fire in the palaver hut. I crossed over to them and squatted beside them. After what seemed like an interminable silence, I burst out: 'Please, help me!'

Slowly, carefully, graciously, Pastor Ndugu took me step by step through the rudiments of the Gospel, reminding me of God's all-sufficient, never-failing grace, of all He had done to rescue and save me, of His infinite condescension in inviting me to be His co-worker, sending me out to Africa as His ambassador. He reminded me of God's promise to indwell and control the lives of His servants, so that we should shine with the goodness of the Lord Jesus, however dark the surrounding darkness.

And then he said: 'Helen, do you know what's wrong with you? We can see so much Helen that we cannot see Jesus.'

I swallowed hard. Almost ruthlessly, and yet lovingly, Pastor Ndugu seemed to dissect my life before my very eyes, pointing out flaws that were so obvious to him, and yet that I thought no one knew about except myself. He exposed me to myself, and it was not a pleasant sight.

Then, ever so simply, he opened his Bible at Paul's letter to the Galatians and read the twentieth verse of the second chapter to me: 'I have been crucified with Christ and I no longer live, but Christ lives in me.'

'That happened when you first came to God, for forgiveness and to be saved from your sin,' he reminded me. 'But, Helen, that needs to be your everyday experience as well.' It is like oiling the bicycle daily, if it is to run well. Having the Hub in place and everything correctly put together is insufficient for smooth functioning. There has to be the oil, as well.

'I see you drink a lot of coffee, Helen,' he continued quietly, apparently changing the conversation, 'and every time someone brings you a mug of coffee, whatever you are doing, you stand with it in your hands, waiting for it to cool down. May I suggest that you pray a short prayer as you wait? "Please, God, cross out my 'I'." '

For me, that was to become my 'oiling' process through many years. 'Please, God, cross out my "I". Help me to see things from the other person's point of view; slow me down so that I can stop and think why they did that irritating thing before getting annoyed with them; show me their needs, and help me to be more interested in meeting their needs than in their meeting my needs.' 'If you then, though you are evil, know how to give good gifts to your children, how much more will your Father in heaven give the Holy Spirit to those who ask him!' (Luke 11:13)

Surely the Holy Spirit is the One who will preserve the relationship between myself and my Saviour, true and pure and vibrant: applying the spiritual 'oil' so that my life will function as God meant it to, and preventing me daily, hourly, from becoming a 'cr-cr' Christian. No prayer can give God greater delight or be more certainly 'according to his will' and therefore to be prayed 'in his name', than that short one: 'Please, God, cross out my "I", so that others see and hear Jesus in and through me, instead of myself.' If my sole desire is that my relationship to my Lord and Saviour should be close, real and vital at all times, God will undoubtedly overrule every other outward circumstance that seeks to attack my peace of mind and to break my relationship with God. He will see to the smooth running of that which He Himself has created, to achieve His perfect purpose.

2

The Yoke: the Practice of our Relationship with God

Make me a captive, Lord,
　and then I shall be free;
Force me to render up my sword,
　And I shall conqueror be.
I sink in life's alarms
　When by myself I stand;
Imprison me within Thine arms,
　And strong shall be my hand.

My heart is weak and poor
　Until it Master find:
It has no spring of action sure,
　It varies with the wind;
It cannot freely move
　Till Thou hast wrought its chain;
Enslave it with Thy matchless love,
　And deathless it shall reign.

My power is faint and low
　Till I have learned to serve:
It wants the needed fire to glow,
　It wants the breeze to nerve;
It cannot drive the world
　Until itself be driven;
Its flag can only be unfurled
　When Thou shalt breathe from heaven.

My will is not my own
   Till Thou hast made it Thine;
If it would reach the Monarch's Throne
   It must its crown resign:
It only stands unbent
   Amid the clashing strife,
When on Thy bosom it has leant,
   And found in Thee its life.

George Matheson (1842–1906)

The fact that a wheel needs a hub at its centre in order to function correctly and fulfil its purpose has been used as an allegory of the primary spiritual essential that each of us be rightly related to God.

We now need to pursue this thought further, that we may realise the importance not only of the existence of that relationship, but also of the practical outworking of it in our everyday lives. These two aspects of the truth will help towards our understanding of 'Living Fellowship' with God.

Recognising, then, that the first essential in the lives of each of us is that we be rightly related to God, let us visualise this as the first side of a triangle:

GOD

MYSELF

To understand how this relationship is to be worked out in the practicalities of everyday life, rather than continue with the allegory of the wheel, we will take a symbol from the teaching of the Lord Jesus Himself. Jesus taught His disciples, when they returned from their first mission full of stories of apparent success: 'Come to me, all you who are weary and burdened, and I will give you rest. Take my yoke upon you, and learn from me, for I am gentle and humble in heart, and you will find rest for your souls. For my yoke is easy and my burden is light' (Matt. 11:28–30).

We will take the yoke as our first symbol, that it may teach.us how God wants us to live as a consequence of being rightly related to Him. In later chapters, we shall think of different symbols to help us come to grips with how God wants us to live as a consequence of our right relationships, firstly with other people, and secondly with the world around us. In each of the three symbols, we shall discover there is an inherent element of sacrifice – part of our former 'natural' way of life that we will have to surrender if we would enter into a new 'spiritual' way of life – and also an element of paradox as is so common in the Scriptures. Our first symbol, the yoke, speaks to us of submissive obedience, and it will become obvious that we will have to 'sacrifice' our natural desire for self-sufficiency. The paradox is that in submission to Christ, contrary to any expectation of subservience, there is actually perfect freedom.

GOD

Submission
to the
yoke

MYSELF

Just what is a yoke? We no longer see this piece of farm equipment in everyday use. In the early part of this century it was common to see a farmer turning the soil in his fields, with the ploughshares pulled by two oxen. The patient, strong beasts would have been yoked together by a seemingly heavy wooden beam laid across their shoulders, to which the blades were harnessed. The beam had two well-smoothed notches carefully etched out of the undersurface, which fitted snugly round the necks of the two animals. As they walked in step, side by side, they hardly noticed the yoke. It did not chafe or irritate them; its weight became negligible as they worked together in perfect harmony.

However, had you watched a young bullock being broken in to carry the yoke, you would have thought the beam was an instrument of torture! Certainly, it looked heavy and imprisoning, and if the younger animal resisted in any way, refusing to go in the same direction or at the same pace as the older beast, seeking to impose its own will rather than submit to team work, then the yoke was restrictive and the creature's neck could be chafed. But as long as they walked together and pulled equally, the yoke proved light and easy to bear.

All of which was well known to those to whom the Saviour spoke those words of comfort.

The yoke is, without doubt, a symbol of servanthood. The first thing we have to accept is that the Christian life is to be one of service. The spiritual yoke will be laid upon us by our Master, to increase our ability to serve Him and work for Him. Paul, writing to the Church in Rome, made this truth very clear to the early Christians. In chapter 6, he writes, 'You used to be slaves to sin' (Rom. 6:17), reminding us that initially, before our new birth and adoption into God's family by His grace and through the merits of His Son's vicarious death for us on Calvary, we all served Satan. Then, when we were saved and had received from God's hands our wonderful redemption and the right to be called children of God, Paul continues, 'You ... have become slaves to righteousness' (verse 18). The servant-status did not change: the only change was the Master whom we served. God created us that we might love Him, and have fellowship with Him; and that love could only be shown by obedience to His commands and submission to His authority. Thus we were created to be His servants. All that is clearly stated in Genesis chapter 2, and throughout the Old and New Testaments. 'You are free to eat from any tree in the garden; but you must not eat from the tree of the knowledge of good and evil, for when you eat of it, you will surely die' (Gen. 2:16–17).

Our first ancestors were given one simple command, in order to give them the opportunity to show their love for their Creator-God by obedience. Did they begin to question, 'But why not taste and see? Is the fruit very different? Would it really matter?'·

And the devil sized up the situation and threw in his wily temptation, by subtly changing the word of God, 'Did God really say, "You must not eat from any tree in the garden"?' (Gen. 3:1) The woman explained that they might eat of all except the one, but that one was forbidden to them. If they ate of it, they would die. 'You will not surely die,' Satan reasoned, 'for God knows that when you eat of it . . . you will be like God, knowing good and evil' (Gen. 3:4–5).

And they chose what they thought was freedom, freedom from God's 'unreasonable restriction', freedom from the need to submit and to serve. This first sin, in the Garden of Eden, was the sin of insubordination: a refusal to obey the voice of God, a refusal by man to submit his will to God's will. Self asserting itself, man's will demanded its right to make its own decision and go its own way. And our ancestors became, in that instant, slaves of Satan, servants of sin. They found no freedom, only greater restrictions, sin now having dominion over them – the 'tyranny of sin', as the hymn-writer expresses it.

When the divine Son of God was born into this world, He lived a life of unquestioning obedience to His Father. He sought always to do His Father's will, to think

His thoughts, speak His words, perform the actions of His purposes; as He Himself said, seeking 'always to please Him'. In the Garden of Gethsemane, falling on His face before His heavenly Father, Christ Jesus prayed with strong tears, 'My Father, if it is possible, may this cup be taken from me. Yet not as I will, but as you will' (Matt. 26:36–9).

> . . . Christ Jesus . . . being in very nature God,
>   did not consider equality with God
>   something to be grasped,
> but made himself nothing,
>   taking the very nature of a servant,
>   being made in human likeness.
> And being found in appearance as a man,
>   he humbled himself
>   and became obedient to death—even
>   death on a cross!
>
>   (Phil. 2:6–8)

For just as through the disobedience of the one man the many were made sinners, so also through the obedience of the one man the many will be made righteous (Rom. 5:19).

Our Lord Jesus Christ gave willing, submissive obedience to His Father throughout His whole earthly life, never once rebelling or seeking His own way or choosing an easier path for Himself than that chosen for Him by His Father, even when this included the cruel death by crucifixion. In doing this, He fulfilled all the obedience that we humans have failed to give to God.

Once we reject the servant-role for which God created us and seek to order our own lives, things go wrong. We cannot support the master-role because we were not created for it. When we became sons and daughters of God, this new relationship should have caused us to revert instantaneously to our rightful servant-status, in submission to the will of our heavenly Father.

But did we? Do we, in actual fact, daily commit ourselves to a renewed submission to His will, and therefore, logically, to a rejection of any inferred right to self-determination? Do not most of us actually continue to live according to our own desires, following our own wills and whims? Do I not usually want my own way, and then ask God to bless my plans? Do we not all tend to reason out what we think will work in our varying sets of circumstances, rather than literally submitting ourselves to an obedience to the Word of God?

To submit is to place ourselves voluntarily under the authority of another; to a Christian, that is specifically to place oneself under the authority of God and His written Word. This is very different from being subjected to the will of another. That is when someone forcibly and determinedly places himself over another, and compels them to obey his will whether they want to or not. God never subjects us to His will, but always seeks that we should submit ourselves to Him, as trusting children to a loving Father.

Am I willing to will to be under God's authority, seeking to obey in every particular His written Word and to please Him in every part of my life? Do I will to give unquestioning obedience to God? I talk about loving God; I may sing about loving God; but in reality, do I actually love Him to the extent that I am prepared to obey Him – even if I don't always understand why He has made certain laws and imposed certain apparent restrictions? Am I so convinced of His unlimited love for me that I know that any such restriction must be for my good, and should therefore be embraced whole-heartedly? 'Whoever has my commands and obeys them, he is the one who loves me' (John 14:21).

So spoke our Saviour Himself, so I dare not talk about loving Him unless I am honestly seeking, in every possible way, to obey His least as well as His greatest command. That obedience, and that alone, shows the reality of my love. To say or sing that I love Him, and yet blatantly to disobey one of His clear commands, is to act a lie.

To whom do we submit?

Why are we so chary of even the idea of submission? Have we never realised that it is the great Almighty God who asks for our submission? Isaiah exalts Him to His true magnificence:

> 'Here is your God!'
> See, the Sovereign Lord comes with power,
>   and his arm rules for him . . .
> He tends his flock like a shepherd:
>   He gathers the lambs in his arms
> and carries them close to his heart;
>   he gently leads those that have young.

> Who has measured the waters in the
>   hollow of his hand,
>   or with the breadth of his hand
>   marked off the heavens?
> Who has held the dust of the earth in a
>   basket,
>   or weighed the mountains on the
>   scales
>   and the hills in a balance?
> Who has understood the mind of the
>   Lord,
>   or instructed him as his counsellor?
> Whom did the Lord consult to
>   enlighten him,
>   and who taught him the right way?
> Who was it that taught him knowledge
>   or showed him the path of
>   understanding?

Surely the nations are like a drop in a
    bucket;
  they are regarded as dust on the
    scales;
  he weighs the islands as though they
    were fine dust . . .

He sits enthroned above the circle of
    the earth,
  and its people are like grasshoppers.
He stretches out the heavens like a
    canopy,
  and spreads them out like a tent to
    live in,
He brings princes to naught
  and reduces the rulers of this world to
    nothing . . .

Lift your eyes and look to the heavens:
  Who created all these?
He who brings out the starry host one
    by one,
  and calls them each by name.
Because of his great power and mighty
    strength,
  not one of them is missing.

The Lord is the everlasting God,
  the Creator of the ends of the earth.
He will not grow tired or weary,
  and his understanding no-one can
    fathom.

(Isa. 40:9–28)

Paul brings to us this same tremendous awesome wonder
in the presence of the Almighty, the Sovereign Lord God,
when he writes his first letter to the Christians at Corinth:

'No eye has seen,
  no ear has heard,
no mind has conceived
  what God has prepared for those who
    love him'—

but God has revealed it to us by his Spirit.
  The Spirit searches all things, even the deep
things of God (1 Cor. 2:9–10).

To enjoy the deep fellowship to which we now have
access, as children of God, demands that we develop a
sense of the Presence of the Eternal as the most important and vivid fact in our daily lives. Every occurrence,
every act, every word, must be seen to be part of God's
plan for our individual lives. It must become a habit,
consciously or subconsciously, to relate every event,
big or little, to God, realising it to be part of His plan
and purpose. It must become instinctive to ask Him for
understanding whenever a doubt or question arises in
our minds.

That is what 'being yoked to Christ' means in practical everyday language. I must not allow the devil to
separate my living and thinking from my realisation of
belonging to God. My whole being is to be linked to
Him in a very tangible and inescapable way. I am to
be bound to Him by His yoke. I must pull with Him,
or else expect to be bruised.

Evelyn Underhill was once invited to give three
addresses at a conference of Anglican ministers. Subse-
quently, her notes were printed in a small book entitled
Concerning the Inner Life (Methuen, 1926). 'The very
first requisite for a teacher of spiritual truths,' she stated,
'is that his own inner life should be maintained in a
healthy state, and his contact with God be steady and
true.'

She went on to say that because those ministers were
all employed full-time in what are called 'religious
activities', and were being constantly drained of their

spiritual resources, they often had less, rather than more, time to devote to caring for their own inner life with God. 'The minister often cannot see the forest because he is attending so faithfully to the trees.' So what did she suggest as the remedy? 'Firstly, a conception, as clear and rich and deep as you are able to get it, of the splendour of God.'

This will surely demand of us that we keep our eyes on God, rather than on humanity. Do we not need in these days to return to a stress on awe for God, rather than on service by humanity, as we relate to our heavenly Father?

There has been a trend in recent years towards a social Christianity: towards an emphasis on bright ethical piety, where service is more important than awe; yet this is proving insufficient to meet the needs of the pain and suffering of humanity. There are some who would even dare to scoff at (or at least, to belittle the importance of) awe, as this manifests itself in a growing hunger for prayer and holiness. Such scoffing, however expressed, with humour or sarcasm, can cause great soul distress to the one who is seeking to walk ever more closely in fellowship with the Lord. It may even cause one to wonder if one is odd, out of step with all the rest of Christendom and so, perhaps, wrong.

However, the more we mix with the world around us, the more we find people who are 'tortured, twisted, driven souls' (as Underhill expressed it), who long for a draught of fresh water from the deep springs of eternal life. And for their sake we must not allow ourselves to be ridiculed or otherwise cheated out of our true inheritance. We need to give all possible time and energy to deepening and increasing our love for God and to finding the infinite joy and delight of surrendering our all to Him, in awed submission. That is how we can become contagious Christians through whom others can catch a sense of the greatness of the love of God and of His power to satisfy their deepest need.

Have we captured the wonder and splendour of the majesty of our God with the imagination of an artist? Is our sense of awe in the presence of our divine Lover growing keener and deeper? In our prayer life, have we reached that stage when we only seek God, in and for Himself, and not for any of His benefits? Sometimes as we bow before Him in total inner silence, with a deep desire to worship Him and to hear His still small voice, there may come over us an almost shattering conviction of the very presence of God Himself. No longer will we even seek to worship Him, let alone to bother Him with our small and insignificant problems, or to ask His help for success in our little bit of ministry – God fills our horizon.

My goal is God Himself, not joy, nor peace,
Nor even blessing, but Himself, my God;
'Tis His to lead me there, not mine, but His,
'At any cost, dear Lord, by any road!'

Fanny Brook, *Hymns of Consecration and Faith*

Suddenly nothing matters, but God – not even my relationship to God, not even the job which God has given me to do. In the complete silence, the very Presence of the Almighty, His greatness and majesty and awesomeness so grip that it would seem to overwhelm one.

Ignatius Loyola said, 'Man was created for this end – to praise, reverence and serve the Lord his God.' Our first duty is adoration; our second awe; and only our third is service. As we seek to maintain a constant sense of the presence of the Eternal, every act and thought of our lives will be transformed into worship and adoration. Then we can make this real to those whom we serve.

We are to be agents to the world of the supernatural, living in the plane of the heavenlies, even though our feet are on this earth. Ordinary folk hurry and hustle through life, with all its daily demands, opportunities and obligations, obsessed by the ceaseless chain of activities and, for the most part, oblivious to, or forgetful of, the mystery that surrounds them. The fact of *life* passes them by; they forget to notice that they are alive. They fail to be awed by the power of life and by its responsibilities. They entirely miss the wealth of spiritual reality that constantly and intimately surrounds them.

We cannot afford to ignore or to forget this; it is the very essence of being alive, of being conscious of life within us. The whole meaning of Christianity is that we live our lives in the presence of Almighty God – that is to say, in fellowship with Him. Have we, each one of us, apprehended this truth? Do we live constantly in the presence of the spaceless and unchanging God, the God who not only blazes on our spiritual horizons, but who also lives intimately within the world of present-tense commonplace events?

Equally, our prayer life must become utterly theocentric, centred on God in all His beauty and majesty and power, and in no way dependent on our own subjective feelings and varying needs, nor even on the feelings and needs of those whom we seek to serve. 'Is my God big enough?' someone has asked, or have I tried to contract Him down to a size I can comprehend and 'manage'? God should fill my horizons! He should be vaster than all my comprehension, yet wholly filling my understanding. Do I perpetually turn to Him, losing myself and my petty interests in His vast unfathomable love and greatness, and refusing to allow even the most pressing work or practical problems to distract me from Him? That is fellowship with the Almighty, and only thus will I keep alive the awed sense of the mysteries that I long to share with others.

In the nineteenth century, Mother Janet Stuart used to say to her novices, 'Think glorious thoughts of God ... then (and only then) serve Him with a quiet mind.' Not controversial thoughts; not dry academic thoughts; not anxious, worried thoughts; not narrow, conventional thoughts; not critical or vindictive or self-assertive thoughts; no! Awed and delighted thoughts, glorious thoughts of the great Reality and Holiness that is GOD, incomprehensible and yet revealed deep within us by the work of the blessed Holy Spirit. May we 'keep our windows open towards God' at all times and in all places!

Our inner life must be an ever-deepening awareness of this great and wonderful God. The sense of the presence of God, immeasurably beyond us, will keep us in a constant attitude of humble awe. Yet He is so closely with us that we can cling to Him in trust and loyal love.

This transcendent God is the One who invites us to be yoked to Him!

This God became our Saviour. He, the Almighty, the Majestic, the Creator:

> . . . made himself nothing,
>   taking the very nature of a servant,
>   being made in human likeness . . .
>   he humbled himself
>   and became obedient to death – even
>   death on a cross!
>
> (Phil. 2:6–8)

This God made Himself a little lower than the angels, so that He might taste death for everyone. God made the author of our Salvation perfect through suffering, and then crowned Him with glory and honour. Although He was a Son, He learned obedience from what He suffered and, once made perfect, He became the source of eternal salvation for all who obey Him (Heb. 2:7–10, 5:8–9).

The transcendent God of Glory and the humble God of our Salvation – this is the One who invites us to be yoked to Him, and thus to learn of Him and so to become like Him.

Let us see this phrase: 'Take my yoke upon you and

learn of me,' in its context, as Christ spoke these words shortly after delivering the Sermon on the Mount.

In that profoundly simple Sermon, the Master-Preacher taught us that we were to be perfect as the Father was perfect (Matt. 5:48). How can we be perfect as He was? In Matt. 5:38–48 He reveals Himself to us as being perfect in meekness, commanding us not to resist evil; He was perfect in generosity, commanding us to give to the one who asks us; He was perfect in compassion, commanding us to love our enemies and pray for those who persecute us. Humanly speaking, all this is beyond us, beyond our wildest dreams, totally impossible, too other-worldly, we think, ever to work in this hurly-burly world in which we live. And yet, as we walk in step with Him, He will show us that it is possible, teaching us what it means in daily practice.

He continued (in chapter 6) to teach us to do our giving, praying and fasting 'in secret' – not ostentatiously so as to be seen of men, but 'in secret', just for God's eyes, just a whisper in God's ear, listening to Him, being with Him, loving Him. Thus, our treasure will be in heaven, and we will have a single-eye on eternal values.

Jesus went on to teach that He had power to forgive sins; that He came to seek the lost and to call sinners to repentance; that He had compassion on all manner of people, rich and poor, high caste and outcast. Before He sent His disciples out to minister as He had been ministering, He warned them of the troubles that lay ahead for them: the loneliness, hatred, persecution that they should expect to meet. Yet when they came back from their first endeavours, they bragged about their success! That is when He said to them: 'Take my yoke upon you and learn of me' (Matt. 11:29).

This is the means He gave them to fulfil the former command, 'Be perfect, therefore, as your heavenly father is perfect.'

The great transcendent God of all creation and glory

calls us to come to Him and to accept that His yoke be placed upon us.

The humble, submissive Son of God, in complete obedience to His Father, shows us the way to come and to accept to be yoked to Him so that we may learn of Him.

The whole tenor of the teaching of the Holy Spirit through the Scriptures is an appeal to us to renounce our own stubborn wills and to submit to God's 'good, pleasing and perfect will', taking God at His word and coming to Him in glad acceptance of His yoke, which, being placed upon us, will enable us to learn of Him.

Why do we need to submit to the yoke?

Submission is essential if we are to fulfil the destiny for which we were created. We were created in the mind of God before He had even laid the foundation of the world, to be 'containers'. Containers need to be filled, if they are to function. God's plan was that we should be filled with His Holy Spirit and so reveal godliness. This demands that we agree to be emptied of self first, so as to be filled with Him. That is the essence of submission, replacing the self with the Christ, replacing my will with His will.

We were not created to be *self*-revealers, like a container saying, 'Look at the beauty of the pattern imprinted on me!' Some of us are so busy seeking a good self-image, either in our own eyes or in the eyes of others – satisfied with our selfhood, as a mere container, without really considering that which indwells us – that we lose the very point of our existence. We were created to 'contain' God so that, perhaps despite the container, perhaps by ignoring the container, others might come to know the contents of our vessel. 'We have this treasure in jars of clay to show that this all-surpassing power is from God and not from us' (2 Cor. 4:7).

We were not created to be *self*-assertive, like a container saying, 'Choose me! See how good and well-proportioned and attractive a vessel I am! Look at the sparkle of the liquid in me!', but rather to be un*self*-conscious, as an overflowing container where no one can see the container, or even think of the container, but only of the overflowing contents.

The Bible uses many illustrations to emphasise this truth. In the verse above, Paul tells us that we were created to be 'jars of clay' carrying the 'treasure', that is the Lord Jesus Christ. Thirsty people are not interested in the colour, shape or texture of the jar, so long as it is clean and does not leak. What they crave is the living water that the jar contains to slake their spiritual thirst.

Again, in 1 Corinthians 3:16, Paul calls us 'temples' indwelt by God the Holy Spirit: 'Don't you know that you yourselves are God's temple and that God's Spirit lives in you?'

We are actually invited to be the home of God Himself. A temple, despite all possible ornate glory in its construction, despite all paint and varnish on its exterior, all carving and carpeting in its interior, is meaningless and unable to function if its doors are padlocked and no one allowed to enter or to worship there. As God's temples, we are created to be lived in, indwelt by God. Time and again in the Scriptures, God has promised to be our God and to live in our midst: 'I will live with them and walk among them, and I will be their God and they will be my people' (2 Cor. 6:16). 'If anyone loves me, he will obey my teaching. My Father will love him, and we will come to him and make our home with him' (John 14:23); and it is His presence that makes our temples worthy of their existence.

In 1 Corinthians 12, Paul uses another illustration to convey the same truth – that we are to be members of a body. The Church is to be considered as Christ's Body, and we are all members of that Body: fingers, hands, arms; toes, feet, legs; eyes and ears, lips and mouths. A finger apart from a body has no meaning, no life, no usefulness. Lips without a head to command their manner of speech cannot function as they were designed to do. We need to be part of Him, to have His life-force coursing through our blood vessels, controlling our nervous impulses, directing our actions and reactions, to enable us to fulfil the meaning of our existence.

Our Lord Jesus Christ Himself called us 'branches' and Himself the Vine: 'I am the vine; you are the branches. If a man remains in me and I in him, he will bear much fruit; apart from me you can do nothing' (John 15:5).

A branch, cut off from the trunk, withers and dies and is cast out to be burned. It is useless. It cannot bear fruit and, if dried and warped, it cannot be used for building or for carving. It has no strength nor life apart from the living sap that it should contain.

Each illustration brings us back to the one underlying truth: we are created to be containers. As such, we are always the lesser, relating to the greater, as a vessel relates to its contents. If we do not submit to being a container and being filled with that which is of greater value than ourselves, then we cannot fulfil the role for which God made us.

Secondly, submission is the only way we have to express our love for God. God created us in His own image, to be to the praise of His glory, and to worship, *love* and serve Him. In the Garden of Eden, God gave man everything he needed to live in happiness and harmony with Himself. He surrounded man with all the beauty of His creation. But as God wanted His creatures to love Him, He had to give them the ability to choose to do so. Love that is obligatory is not love. A robot cannot love because it cannot choose, and the very essence of love is that the lover chooses to love.

I remember clearly one Saturday afternoon at Nebo-bongo. I was ironing the children's Sunday clothes on the verandah of my home. A happy crowd of orphan children were playing in the courtyard. Suddenly, for no apparent reason, one little fellow separated himself from the rest, ran up to me, threw his arms round my legs and blurted out: 'Mummy, I do love you!' I bent down to kiss him, my eyes suddenly full of tears. He ran back to the crowd, wholly unconscious of what his little act had meant to me. He didn't have to tell me of his love. He didn't even have to love me. I would still love him, feed and clothe and care for him. It was the impulsive action of pure love. It was the result of free choice and, as such, it was infinitely precious to me.

So God created us with free will in order that we could choose to love Him. But having chosen to love Him, how could we then express that love to Him? God only gave us one way to express love – by obedience. He gave to Adam and Eve one simple command, that they might have something to obey, and so a means to show their love. Pointing to one tree among the thousands, God said to them: 'You must not eat from the tree of the knowledge of good and evil, for when you eat of it, you will surely die' (Gen. 2:17).

If they truly loved God and wanted some way to express that love, God had given them the means: by obedience to His will. They would not eat of that tree. They might wonder why not. They might even speculate as to what 'death' meant. There could be questions in their mind as to the reason for the command: but true love would overrule everything else, and they would not eat of that tree.

To eat was to manifest a greater love for themselves than for God. It would be a way of self-assertion, demonstrating their 'right' to choose for themselves, to do things their own way, to disobey, and so, their 'right' to reject the need to submit. In other words, they would be rejecting the concept that they were containers, with no inherent rights.

In such a way, I also have been invited by Almighty God to submit to His will, and to cooperate with Him in the fulfilment of His purposes. I am asked to accept from His hands the right to be an earthen jar with the inestimable privilege of being filled with the Spirit of God and used as His ambassador. He invites me to love Him. To express that love, He gives me ample opportunity to obey Him, with glad and unquestioning obedience.

God does not insist or force. He does not subject me to His laws. He loves me so deeply that He trusts me with the gift of free will so that I have the ability to choose to love and so to obey Him. He says: 'Whoever has my commands and obeys them, he is the one who loves Me . . . If anyone loves me, he will obey my teaching' (John 14:21–3).

Throughout the Scriptures, obedience is given as the one way pleasing to our Creator God by which we can express to Him our love, and such obedience always demonstrates the submission of my will to His.

> 'To obey is better than sacrifice,
>   and to heed is better than the fat of
>   rams.'

> (1 Sam. 15:22)

Thirdly, submission is the only way by which I can be released from the bondage of my self-life. By this means I can enter wholly into the liberty of the God-filled life for which I was created. This surely is what Paul teaches us in the sixth chapter of Romans. Three times in as many verses, he points out that by our baptism we have entered into Christ's death. Three times he tells us that our old way of life – the life of self-dominance and self-assertion, a life where each of us claims our rights to ourselves and our choices, a life of total self-centredness – must be committed to death. This is the one 'right' that we have: to choose voluntarily to hand over our self-life to death. I must, deliberately and publicly, declare that my self be crucified and buried with Christ.

Is this not how Christ submitted to His Father through-out His earthly life? He went to death on the Cross as a voluntary offering for sin. 'Unless a grain of wheat falls to the ground and dies, it remains only a single seed.

But if it dies, it produces many seeds' (John 12:24). The 'grain of wheat' was buried in the ground and died, that it might bring forth a wonderful harvest. It died to itself, its independent self-life, in order to give its life to others. So Christ spoke in parable of what He was about to do for us: 'God made Him [Jesus] who had no sin to be sin for us, so that in him we might become the righteousness of God' (2 Cor. 5:21).

We must carefully continue to follow Paul in his orderly presentation of the facts in that sixth chapter of his letter to the Romans. In verse 4, he says, 'Just as Christ was raised from the dead through the glory of the Father, we too may live a new life.'

In verse 5 he tells us that we shall be 'united with him in his resurrection'. Here we see the new life replacing the old; life coming out of the death process. This is the eternal life of God that is imparted to us at our second birth. It is a God-centred and God-glorifying life that takes over from our old self-centred and self-interested life.

We have to submit to the death process if we would know the life process. We have to agree that our old life must die with Christ, as He died on the Cross, so that His resurrection life can function in us. In that death, when 'our old self [is] crucified with Him,' the self-centredness is dealt with and Christ is enthroned. The result is that we need 'no longer be slaves to sin – because anyone who has died has been freed from sin' (Rom. 6:6–7). We can now reckon on Christ's death in our place and His resurrection life indwelling us, to replace our self-life with His God-life.

Paul continues his reasoned argument in verse 12:

> Therefore do not let sin reign in your mortal body so that you obey its evil desires. Do not offer the parts of your body to sin, as instruments of wickedness, but rather offer yourselves to God, as those who have been brought from death to life; and offer the parts of your body to him as

instruments of righteousness. For sin shall not be your master . . . (Rom. 6:12–14).

That is to say, by a conscious act of will we refuse the right of self to dominate. We no longer yield to the lusts of our nature, nor submit to the tyranny of Satan and his lies, nor to our sense of our rights. We no longer acknowledge self on the throne but, deliberately *de*throning self, we yield ourselves voluntarily to God and to His righteousness, equally deliberately *en*throning Christ.

We have chosen to change Masters! We are still servants – we were created to be servants, to be containers – but now we serve God, and not self and Satan. 'Don't you know that when you offer yourselves to someone to obey him as slaves, you are slaves to the one whom you obey?' (Rom. 6:16)

If I submit to the devil and myself, I am under the domination of sin, which leads me to spiritual death. But if I submit to the authority of God, I am under His dominion, which leads me to eternal life. 'Though you used to be slaves to sin, you wholeheartedly obeyed the form of teaching to which you were entrusted. You have been set free from sin and have become slaves to righteousness' (Rom. 6:17–18). To obey wholeheartedly is to give voluntary submission to Christ.

We were slaves . . . we become slaves. The status does not change, but the Master does! Our only choice is to whom we submit. We must submit to one or the other. As I submit to self, I remain under the domination of self. The only way to escape and to be released from myself is to submit to God and accept His dominion over me. 'Just as you used to offer the parts of your body in slavery to impurity . . . so now offer them in slavery to righteousness leading to holiness' (Rom. 6:19).

Why should we submit? There is no other way to fulfil God's planned purpose for our lives as containers. There is no other way to express to God our love for Him other than by obedience. There is no other way by which I can be freed from the burden and bondage of my self and my sinfulness, and enter into the glorious liberty He has prepared for me as His servant.

How do we submit to God?

'Come to me, all you who are weary and burdened, and I will give you rest' (Matt. 11:28).

Let us remind ourselves of the difference between subjection and submission. Subjection is the imposition of the will of another over me, without any choice on my part; submission is the voluntary act of putting myself under the control of another. As I accept the fact that I was created to be a container, and as such I can be filled either by the spirit of this world or by the Holy Spirit of God, then I can look forward to the result that accrues if I choose the latter and submit myself to God's authority. I have to make a willed decision to submit to the crucifixion of myself, so that I can say with Paul, 'I have been crucified with Christ and I no longer live, but Christ lives in me. The life I live in the body, I live by faith in the Son of God, who loved me and gave himself for me' (Galatians 2:20).

Once we submit, then Christ will indwell and fill us. But we have to ask God to empty us of *self*, and then fill us with *Him*self.

I remember watching the children in our Nebobongo village, early in the morning, going down to the spring, each to fill the family's water-pot. They knew the rules very well. As they neared the spring they should throw out all that remained of yesterday's water, swilling out the pot as they did so. Then they could allow a little fresh water to pour into their vessel. Once again, they must swill it round thoroughly and throw it out. This would be repeated two or three times until there were no leaves, no dust, no foreign bodies left in the vessel, and until the vessel itself became chilled with the fresh early morning water. Now they were ready to fill the pot to the brim, place a newly cut banana leaf over the top, balance it carefully on the top of the head and start the clamber homewards.

But children will be children all the world over. Their interest in filling the water-pots with fresh clean water for the new day was scanty! The job had to be done as fast as possible, in order to gain their release from parental authority and freedom for a game of football! Down to the spring they would rush, push their jar under the flowing water, fill it to the brim and scramble for home.

Slipping in quietly, they would lower the jar to the ground, hoping not to be heard, and out again into the sunshine, as fast as they could make it!

Caught by a suspicious mother, they would rarely escape without both a scolding and being sent back again to the spring for fresh water.

'You didn't clean the jar today,' mother would remonstrate.

'Oh, I did, I did,' from the hapless youngster.

'No,' she would go on, 'the water is warm, and the dust of yesterday floats on the surface! Go back and fetch me clean fresh water!'

Is it not like that in our spiritual lives? We may try to mix the new fresh life of the Spirit of God with our old stale life of the spirit of the world, a bit of each, keeping, as it were, one foot in each world. But it does not work like that. The Spirit of God cannot and will not mix with the spirit of the world. We have to ask God to empty us of the old, in order to fill us with the new. I must willingly and voluntarily choose to exchange my old life for the new. There are so many Scriptures that teach us this truth:

> God made Him [Jesus] who had no sin to be sin for us, so that in Him we might become the right-eousness of God. (2 Cor. 5:21).

> Jesus Christ, who gave himself for us to redeem

us from all wickedness and to purify for himself a people that are his very own, eager to do what is good (Titus 2:13–14).

I must maintain this position daily. Following the initial act of will, when I accept that I am created to contain and not to self-advertise, there has to be a steady progression and growth.

Then he [Jesus] said to them all: 'If anyone would come after me, he must deny himself, and take up his cross daily and follow Me' (Luke 9:23).

Jesus taught them, when they prayed, to say: 'Our Father . . . give us today our daily bread' (Matt. 6:11).

As it is written:

'For your sake we face death all day long;
    we are considered as sheep to be slaughtered.'

(Rom. 8:36)

'I die every day,' testified Paul (1 Cor. 15:31).

Whom does Christ call to this life of submission? Go back to our first text in this section. 'Come to me, all you who are weary and burdened' (Matt. 11:28). He calls 'all who are weary': all, that is, who are striving to please Him, struggling to deny self, lonely, without a human companion to share the load; 'all who are burdened': all who are shouldering great burdens for others, discouraged at the unresponsiveness of the majority, hearts burdened for the unsaved and unreached of family, community, country and world. And what does He promise to all such who come to Him? 'I will give you rest' (Matt. 11:28).

How we all long for that deep rest of heart and mind, that only God can give! Jesus promised to give His disciples His peace – unmeasured, infinite, constant, unchanging peace. Peace that will replace the pressures and near-panic and utter weariness that fill so many of us as we labour in our service for God. He meant us to have peace, to be at rest in Him. He never intended that we should be overwhelmed and almost shattered by the vastness of the task to which we are called as His ambassadors. But so often we choose to shoulder the load alone, refusing to submit to Him, refusing to surrender our right to be loners and so refusing to roll the load back on to Him, who is waiting to receive it.

Has He not encouraged us to hand the burdens over to Him? 'Cast all your anxiety on him because he cares for you' (1 Pet. 5:7).

So many great and precious promises He has given us, such as 'I will give you rest.' But what do we have to do to inherit these promises? He Himself tells us clearly. He leaves nothing to chance. 'Take my yoke upon you' (Matt. 11:29).

'Be yoked to Almighty God,' He commands us – inviting us to worship and adore Him, putting Him first in everything.

'Be yoked to the humble obedient Servant-Son,' He invites us – imitating Him who came not to be served but to serve and to give His life as a ransom for many.

'Be yoked in obedience to the Word,' He pleads with us – seeking out His commands that we may be wholly obedient to them.

Is God saying to me, 'Bow your proud neck and your stubborn will, and let Me, Almighty God, place My yoke on you'? Maybe it does look heavy and restraining, like inescapable imprisonment, whilst we remain unbowed in rebellion. Maybe it does look like anything other than rest, rather a symbol of a hard labour camp, until we give in and accept His authority over us.

And yet, it is as though God were saying to each one of us, 'Be yoked to Me: walk in step with Me. The beam will fall across us both equally and keep us in touch and in step with each other. Let Me lead you captive, and teach and instruct you as we plough together. I promise you, I will do most of the pulling, you only have to cooperate. I'll be responsible for the steering, you only have to follow My lead.'

The Ruanda Mission card of the Forties and Fifties bore first the words 'Not I but Christ', from Galatians 2:20, and then this poem:

> Lord, bend that proud and stiff-necked 'I',
> Help me to bow the neck and die,
> Beholding Him on Calvary
> Who bowed His head for me.

In the capital 'I' on the card there was the picture of a man, stiff and rigid with self-importance, and in the capital 'C' there was the same man, bent and kneeling in prayerful submission. Why do we find it so hard to 'bow the neck and die'? Why do we resist so strongly His patient invitation to submit and accept? 'Take my yoke upon you and learn from me' (Matt. 11:29).

It is as though the Almighty pleads with each one of us in turn, 'I'll be so patient and kind with you. I will lend you all My strength and give you My power. I'll carry the heavy end of the burden. I'll only place on you the little bit that I know you can manage. I'll help you over the rough places and lead you where there is green pasture and running water for your refreshment. I want you to learn to live My way, to think My way, to love My way; and I am willing to teach you everything that pleases Me.'

Do you remember the story of how King David sought to bring the Ark of the Covenant from Kiriath Jearim to Jerusalem? First he tried his own way, and everything went wrong; then he tried the right way, and he succeeded. There is a right and a wrong way of doing all things, and God takes care to show us and teach us this fact in the Bible.

David had discussed his plans with 'the whole assembly' of Israel and they had all agreed with his plans, 'because it seemed right to all the people'.

> They moved the ark of God ... on a new cart, with Uzzah and Ahio guiding it. David and all the Israelites were celebrating with all their might before God, with songs and with harps, lyres, tambourines, cymbals and trumpets.
>
> When they came to the threshing-floor of Kidon, Uzzah reached out his hand to steady the ark; because the oxen stumbled. The Lord's anger burned against Uzzah ... because he had put his hand on the ark (1 Chr. 13).

Uzzah died. David trembled and was filled with fear. And he left the Ark with a family in that place of death, rather than try again.

Some time later, David's heart was again moved by God to bring the Ark to its proper resting place in Jerusalem. But this time he prayed about the matter, and sought in the available Scriptures to discover God's way of doing the task, in order that everything should be right in the eyes of God, rather than merely in the eyes of the people. He discovered that God had commanded that the holy things of the Tabernacle were to be carried on the shoulders of men when they moved camp, and were not to be put on carts, new or old. 'No-one but the Levites may carry the ark of God,' David told all the people, 'because the Lord chose them to carry the ark of the Lord and to minister before him for ever' (1 Chr. 15:2).

David had gathered all the people together, not now to ask them their opinions, but to tell them how the job was to be done:

> You ... are to consecrate yourselves and bring up the ark of the Lord, the God of Israel, to the place I have prepared for it. It was because you,

the Levites, did not bring it up the first time that the Lord our God broke out in anger against us. We did not enquire of Him about how to do it in the prescribed way. So . . . the Levites carried the ark of God with the poles on their shoulders, as Moses had commanded in accordance with the Word of the Lord (1 Chr. 15:12–15; see Exod. 25:14 and Num. 4:15).

As the Ark was borne in triumph to Jerusalem, David and all the people sang and sacrificed all along the route, and God honoured them this time, because they did it in the manner He had commanded them.

The only difference between the two methods employed in the thirteenth and in the fifteenth chapters of the first book of Chronicles, was obedience to the revealed will of God. This must be true for all of us. We must obey God in every detail in submission and humility: this will always be better and more pleasing to God than seeking to offer our sacrifice or praise in some new way of worship or of service, like the 'new cart' David had made for the Ark!

Sometimes the way of obedience may seem very humdrum, ordinary and unexciting – and we could easily think up all sorts of devices and gimmicks to cheer it all up . . . but God has His own perfect plan, and all He asks of us is submissive obedience to Him in love.

When we submit and bend our necks under His yoke, we find His yoke is smooth. It fits us exactly, with no chafing. It makes us want to pull and go with Him. As we break our proud wills and submit in obedience to His gentle will, work becomes a joy instead of drudgery:

> The sacrifices of God are a broken spirit;
> a broken and contrite heart,
> O God, you will not despise.

> (Ps. 51:17)

For this is what the high and lofty One
   says –
   he who lives for ever, whose name is
   holy:
'I live in a high and holy place,
   but also with him who is contrite and
    lowly in spirit,
to revive the spirit of the lowly
   and to revive the heart of the contrite.'

                    (Isa. 57:15)

'Take my yoke upon you and learn from me' is God's command to us for submission. We are to submit to Almighty God in awed reverence. We are to submit to the Saviour in perfect obedience. In submission, we accept that our role is that of servants to obey, and we shall seek to say daily, 'Not my will, but Yours, be done.' We voluntarily place ourselves under the authority of the Word.

Such submission is the only reasonable response of our hearts to His great love, to His eternal mercy, to His amazing call to us to be His co-labourers – it is the only way into His perfect service. 'I beseech you therefore, brethren, by the mercies of God, that ye present your bodies a living sacrifice, holy, acceptable unto God, which is your reasonable service' (Rom. 12:1, AV).

And it is only by such perfect submission to His will that we will find perfect freedom! A paradox maybe, but it is the truth. 'Then you will know the truth, and the truth will set you free . . . the Son sets you free, you will be free indeed' (John 8:32,36).

Am I, are you, living our daily lives in perfect submission to His will? My relationship to God, as an adopted child through the shed blood of Calvary, demands that I submit happily and willingly to Him as my Father as well as my Creator. Have I yielded myself to Him as His love-slave? Will I do so daily through the rest of my life? Only thus can we go out to serve Him in the power of the Spirit.

It is here that we must start. We cannot rightly relate to and therefore have fellowship with our fellow-men if we have not submitted to God's rightful authority over us. Once this submission to the yoke of Christ is fully established in my heart and life, then I can seek to bring others to Him. Our service *for* Christ, as we shall see in subsequent chapters, depends on our submission *to* Christ. We must accept the *yoke* before we can use the *towel*.

PART II

OUR FELLOWSHIP WITH OTHERS

3

Our Relationship with Others: the Spokes

Let us return now to our analogy of the bicycle wheel, as we concentrate in this chapter on the role of the spokes. Each spoke, left to itself, is an almost worthless thing, weak and unable to achieve anything. But, working together in harmony, the spokes can achieve a great deal, transmitting the power from the hub to the rim and so causing the whole wheel to turn and the bicycle to move forward.

These spokes can be considered as an illustration of individuals, each one of us in our different places and circumstances, with our different characters and aptitudes.

Note firstly that the power of the spokes is only manifested when they work together with each other, and not in themselves individually. Life is made up of relationships; all of us have to relate the one to the other, however much we may try individually to remain apart and self-sufficient. God created us to be dependent on each other, to live in communities and not in isolation. We need each other.

On a very basic level, this dependence reveals itself in our need for the 'things' that other people make or procure, things that we have no longer the aptitude either to do without or to make for ourselves, such as saucepans, electric light bulbs, toothpaste or salt

– things we tend to take for granted in our western societies. We also need company in our loneliness, encouragement when the going gets rough, help in our sicknesses. We need people around who can mend and fix, who can direct and manage, who can accept and pay.

Not only are we all dependent on our immediate circle of friends and on the services provided by our immediate community but, in a larger sense, also on the leadership of the country to which we belong, and in turn on the interaction of other nations of the world. Most importantly of all, we are all dependent on our Creator (whether we recognise our dependence or not). He gives us breath, He sustains the universe, He holds all the massive forces of nature in check: in short, He makes life possible.

In like manner, the spokes of the wheel have to relate not only to each other, but also to the hub and to the rim, if the whole is to function effectively.

I well remember a situation that arose in my early years in Africa. The background to this particular story is the perhaps sad fact that the Africans with whom I lived and worked considered that Europeans could do practically anything and everything they wanted done. One day, when I came home from the hospital in mid-afternoon, I found a carton on my verandah filled with bits and pieces and a scrawled note, 'Please, Doctor, could you put my bicycle together for me?'

One could not always buy a bicycle as such in those days but, going to the hardware store, one procured all the parts that went into the making of a bicycle and then, hopefully, put it together.

I was so ignorant about such matters that the first time I went to purchase all that was needed to create a bicycle, I picked up two hubs from the box marked 'Hubs', not realising that back and front hubs were quite different! Recognising my total ignorance of everything to do with cycles (except the elementary art of knowing how to ride them), I had written home to my dear, long-suffering mother and asked her to send me a *Teach-Yourself* book on the subject.

Facing that carton on my verandah, I spread out all the bits of the would-be bicycle and wondered where to start the task of creation. After several fruitless efforts to fix the rims to the spokes, and then the spokes to the hubs to form composite wholes, I sat down to study the textbook in greater detail. Armed with diagrams and dental forceps (mechanical pliers being unavailable at that time) I laid all the parts out again in an orderly fashion, prayed for help and started this time with the hub, instead of the rim. Painstakingly I slipped all the curved tips of the spokes into the obvious small holes waiting for them, alternating them to right and left, on the two sides of each hub. When this was completed, laying the whole on the ground and placing the rims around them, the task of fixing the other end of each spoke correctly into its hole in the rim was soon and satisfactorily completed. The secret had been to start from the hub and work outwards, not the other way round – so relatively simple, even obvious, when one knew the trick!

Is this not a good picture of all that concerns our everyday lives? When, in our own strength, we (as a spoke) try to relate to those others around us (as our little bit of rim), almost invariably things go wrong. Judgments are inevitably made from a self-orientated point of view, with an incomplete knowledge of all the relevant facts. Have you known the situation when your neighbours move away? Their house is put up for sale and you begin to think, 'Who will come next?' If you are the owner of a gentle pussy-cat, you hope fervently they won't be the owners of a large dog. If you are an elderly spinster, you may well pray it will not be a family with rowdy children!

Both reactions are part of our need to relate to our next-door neighbours and yet both are self-centred, taking little thought of the needs of the incoming owners. How are we to achieve the former and avoid the latter?

If the hub is in place first, and the spokes are properly related to it, then the task of relating both hub and spokes to the rim is vastly simpler. It is the point of departure that is important in all relationships, if the individuals involved are to achieve harmony. When Christ is the HUB of my life, then all the other relationships with those around me can be adjusted until the whole functions smoothly and effectively. And it does work – from inside outwards, but not the other way round.

I can look back over twenty years of service on the overseas mission field and, more recently, to almost twenty years of service at the home-end of our mission, and almost every time that I have been involved in a difficult situation or where things have gone badly wrong, whether of my own making or of someone else's, I can see on each occasion a breakdown of relationships. Somebody's 'I' wanted something its own way and would not give in to someone else. Both parties were often sure they were right, blamed the other for all that was wrong, and failed to see the problem through the other person's eyes. The simplest and surest way to resolve such situations was by prayer, each asking for God's forgiveness and power to see the situation from the other's viewpoint. Once one of the two parties was willing to go back to the Hub, the Lord Jesus Christ, and restore a right relationship with Him, then the job of rightly relating to their fellow-man was nine-tenths solved.

God wants us, each one of us, to be content to be a spoke in His wheel of life. However, we have to be the right spoke in the right place at the right time, and not the wrong spoke in the wrong place at the wrong time.

From 1960 to 1964 a very sad situation developed in Zaire, after independence had been granted to the country. The European and National communities drifted apart; each felt unable to trust the other. This was not only true in governmental and administrative departments, but it overflowed into Church life. African pastors were hesitant to trust their missionary colleagues, particularly in financial matters. European missionaries were hesitant to trust their African colleagues, particularly with regard to devolving responsibilities. I found this very hard to accept and spent much time in prayer, asking that the rift be healed and unity restored, with no reference to skin-colour.

In October 1964, ten weeks after the start of the horrific civil war that broke in the country that year, it so happened that I was the first white woman in our area to be brutalised by the rough guerrilla soldiers. After a savage night I was taken to a local commercial centre, to which other European 'foreigners' were rounded up during the following morning. We were then bundled unceremoniously into a truck and driven sixty miles to the local township of Isiro, to stand before a firing squad ... only to be released again when arguing broke out between the various factions of the rebel army. Taken back to our villages, we were held under house arrest during what seemed a long weekend – a weekend for me of pain and fear.

On the following Tuesday evening, the rebels came for us again. Having forced us out of the house and lined us up on the verandah, arguments broke out, in particular because of my bruised and battered face.

'Who made that mess of you?' one of the sergeant majors asked.

'One of your men,' I replied.

Angrily, he struck me and called me a liar. I did not then know that they had been instructed not to touch the white women.

'I'm not,' I responded. 'I can name him,' – which I did.

'All right,' he shouted, 'we'll call a people's court.'

They left the village and an uneasy calm settled over us all ... but not for long. That same night, three of them came back in a pick-up truck. They hauled me out and threw me up into the truck, and drove off into the darkness. Stopping here and there they drove,

almost aimlessly it seemed, through the night. As dawn
was breaking, we entered a village clearing where the
rebels had rounded up all the men of the region, having
instructed them crudely as to their part in a 'people's
court'. I would be interrogated and at a certain point,
in response to a given signal, they were to shout out,
'She's a liar! She's a liar!'

The proceedings were pretty chaotic, but eventually
the sergeant major started to interrogate me as to the
happenings of the previous Thursday night when I
had been 'beaten up and brutalised by the soldiers,'
according to my account. Bruised and battered, hardly
able to see out of badly swollen eyes, scared and feeling
desperately alone, I tried to answer the rapidly fired
questions. I knew I was going to die. The only thing I
did not know was how I would die.

There came the moment when the crowd should have
condemned me. I could not see them, but I could hear,
and I became conscious of a strange and growing sound
– a sound I'd never heard before and probably will
never hear again. Several hundred strong farming men
broke down and wept. Men crying. Suddenly, instead
of seeing me as the hated white foreigner, they saw
me as 'their doctor', one they had learned to love and
respect through the past twelve years of service. They
swept forward, driving the rebel soldiers out of the way,
and took me in their arms and hugged me. 'She's ours.
She's ours,' they kept repeating.

God had answered four years of prayer in that moment!
I had no idea that He might ask me to be part of
the process involved in bringing about that restored
unity. It was as though God whispered to me, 'Can you
accept the suffering now? My purpose is to restore the
unity between the national and foreign communities,
something for which you have prayed so fervently.' He
simply wanted me to be a spoke, in the right place at
the right time, that He might do His work.

Five weeks later, after various other episodes, the
eight Protestant missionaries held under house arrest

at Ibambi were driven by the rebel soldiers seventy miles east to Wamba. There they were imprisoned at the Roman Catholic compound, the two men with the priests in the monastery, and the six women with the nuns in the convent. Fifty-two nuns, nine Belgian women and their six children, six Protestant missionaries – seventy-three white women and children – were herded together, in very cramped quarters.

But even in the midst of so much suffering, God was continuing to work out His perfect plan. For the first fifteen weeks of the rebellion, the Greek community (who controlled all the commercial enterprises in the region) had not suffered interference from the guerrillas, as had the Catholic and Protestant missionaries and the Belgian planters and their families. Almost certainly, considerable sums of money had changed hands, a system not available to those of us working in voluntary organisations. But the cash supply inevitably became exhausted. And the rebel army turned on their erstwhile benefactors, refusing to believe that they were truly unable to continue helping them with food, housing and ammunitions.

So, as had happened to us some weeks previously, the Greek community had been rounded up. They were treated with great brutality – beaten, kicked, trampled on. Brought to Wamba, they were herded, all two hundred of them, into two houses, each built for a single family. One of the women was expecting a baby and she was in great pain. The soldiers were frightened that they had caused 'grievous bodily harm' and, coming to the convent, commanded me, as the only available doctor, to accompany them from our prison to the Greeks' 'prison' to see her.

Fearfully, between two armed men, I walked down the road from the convent to the little township and along the main street to the home of Mr Mitsingas. I had no way of knowing if the soldiers' story was true, or if they were taking me away for their own savage purposes. Arriving at the house, we clambered over and through the crowded Greeks to an inner room, where the groaning woman lay on a bed. The soldiers stayed close beside me all the time. I glanced round the packed house – I knew almost everyone there. For years I had been their doctor – bringing their babies into the world, caring for the sick, operating on those needing surgery. But not one of them now looked up or gave me the slightest sign of recognition. They were overwhelmed and stunned by the calamity that had overtaken them during the previous twenty-four hours.

'Lord, why have You brought me here?' I prayed urgently.

Bending over the woman whom I had been brought to see, I began gently to ask her questions and to examine her. Suddenly I knew what I could do.

The soldiers spoke Lingala and knew a smattering of Swahili, an occasional word of French, but no English and no Greek. So, for the next twenty minutes, we carried on a strange conversation in five languages, something as follows.

'Does it hurt here?' in Lingala, repeated in Swahili, neither of which languages did the woman properly understand. For a third time I said the same words, now in French, and then added in English, 'Men, will you please translate my English words into Greek for your women? I am going to talk to you about Jesus.'

The men duly told the women, in their own language, that the doctor was going to talk to them about Jesus; the soldiers presumed that the English and Greek was a direct translation of what they had heard in Lingala, Swahili and French.

And so we continued, phrase by phrase, three languages dealing with a medical examination and later with prescribed treatment, and two languages telling them as simply as I could, in the limited time available, of the Saviour's death on Calvary in their place that they might know forgiveness of sins.

'I am going to give you some medicine and I want you to take two tablets three times a day, until I can come to see you again,' I said, in our first three languages; and then in English, 'I'm going to pray for you without shutting my eyes. Will you repeat the words in your own hearts?' And as I explained the medicines in detail, so I led them in a quiet prayer of confession of sin, asking for forgiveness and opening their hearts to accept the Saviour's promise of salvation.

When I left that home, still escorted by my two body-guards, everyone looked up at me, a new hope in their eyes, grasping my hands and thanking me for coming. The whole atmosphere had changed. Without doubt, some at least had responded to God's grace.

Back at the convent, exhausted and confused, I asked the Lord, 'Why have these people listened and responded to me on this occasion? Have I not been preaching the Gospel to them for twelve years, and they have never shown the slightest interest?'

'They know what you suffered that Thursday night six weeks ago,' the Lord reminded me. 'And were not some of them also there at the people's court that Tuesday night? Didn't they see your bruised and swollen eyes, your cut and bloody face? If you hadn't suffered that night in late October, maybe they wouldn't have listened today. They would have been tempted to say in their hearts, "What does she know about it?" But because they know that you suffered then, despite all that they have suffered now in these last twenty-four hours I have been able to open their hearts to respond to My love and to listen to your words.'

Just a spoke in the right place at the right time. A spoke that had to relate first to the Hub, and then to the rim, in order to carry strength and power from Hub to rim. God had prepared His 'spoke' in the way that He knew was necessary, so that His power could flow through to meet the specific need of that bit of 'rim' at that particular moment. Nothing in itself, but the spoke became everything needed for the particular job, when rightly related between Hub and rim in the position to which God assigned it.

In 1970, after seventeen years of service in Zaire – a doctor/surgeon, the director of a national paramedical college, a Bible teacher – I suddenly found that my presence at the Evangelical Medical Centre was apparently no longer essential. There were others better qualified than I was to teach anatomy and physiology and the art of nursing. There were others much better qualified than I was to diagnose and treat the patients in the wards and in the operating theatres. There were others, national as well as foreign, better qualified to teach the Bible and lead church services. What, then, did the Church and the Medical Centre want me to do?

They had a very clear and unequivocal answer. Would I mind becoming the office-girl?

'You can type,' they said, and had they spoken English, they would have added, 'You can still make two plus two equal four.'

So I became the office-girl. Six days a week, from 6.30 a.m. to 9.0 p.m. I worked at government reports, student dossiers, course material . . . typing, duplicating, filing. I lived with ink, often in the wrong place! I now had very little contact with the patients in the wards; only a few hours a week in contact with the students in the classrooms; far less contact than previously with workmen and church members. I lived ostensibly in the office.

And I did not like it. I loved being with people, not with paper and ink. I guess I grumbled. Eventually I took my grumbles to the College Board of Directors, in order to seek a replacement in the office so that I could be released back into general circulation.

They listened politely: they prayed earnestly.

Then one of them said to me, 'You know, Doctor, we cannot all be the last link in the chain.'

That was true. I of course wanted to be out in the frontline, preaching and telling people about our Lord and Saviour. As a result, I was not happy that others were now doing that part of the work, while I was relegated (as I saw it) to the background.

'Doctor,' he persisted, 'how many graduates from this college are now working as full-time medical auxiliaries in the north-eastern province of Zaire?'

Part of my job was handling the Medical Centre's statistics. At that time, probably about 120 of our college graduates were working full-time for one of the five missionary societies who cooperated in running the Medical Centre.

'Doctor,' he continued, 'how many patients do they see daily?'

It would be hard to give an accurate figure, but approximately ten to twelve thousand patients might be attending one of the rural clinics or regional hospitals on any one day. My inquisitor's eyes challenged me to suggest that I could not see that number of patients a day by myself, but he did not say so aloud.

'Doctor,' he continued gently, 'how many of those patients come to know the Lord Jesus as their own personal Saviour every week as a result of the preaching of the Gospel by our paramedical graduates in all these dispensaries?'

We realise that numbers cannot tell the whole story, but we do know that possibly some two hundred patients put their trust in the Saviour every week through the ministry of our graduates. Again, I was deeply conscious of the fact that I could not achieve that by my own unaided effort.

'Doctor,' he concluded, 'you know that the government does not allow any of the paramedical workers to do their work unless there is a qualified doctor behind them, carrying the responsibility. Don't you realise that we need your signature?'

I swallowed hard. Seventeen years' intense service on the mission field, and all that was now needed was my signature?

But suddenly I saw it, and laughed out loud! How patient God had been, and how faithful to raise up African colleagues with sufficient wise discernment to tell me the truth! In the eyes of God there was no difference between the importance or value of the work of the senior surgeon or most outstanding preacher, and that of the motor-mechanic who kept the ambulance on the road or the office-girl who signed the letters and sent reports to the government. All God asks of us is that each one be willing to be a spoke, in the right place at the right time to do the right job well.

If at that time I had still been doing regular surgery, or still teaching first-year anatomy and physiology, I would have been the wrong spoke in the wrong place at the wrong time – preventing those who were ready to take over the leadership and running of the medical services from doing the jobs for which they had been trained.

Another quite different situation comes to mind. It was several years later, in 1976, when on a deputation tour for our mission in the United States of America, that I found I had a lump. As a doctor I was fairly sure of the diagnosis, believing that I had the beginnings of a probably-malignant tumour. It was four months before I could, conveniently, take time off to go to hospital and have the required treatment.

After I had had the necessary surgery, several friends wrote letters of encouragement, but in many I sensed an unwritten question, 'Why has God allowed this to happen to you? Haven't you been through enough already? Isn't He using you just now in His programme to encourage others to become missionaries, both through the spoken and also the written word?'

When I first became aware of my need for surgery I had perhaps asked God such questions myself, but He had answered me very clearly. 'Can you not trust Me?' He seemed to say to me. 'I do know what I am doing and I have a plan. All I ask of you is the loan of your body.'

In the months and years subsequent to the operation, as I went for check-ups, I found a simple explanation as to why God had asked me to accept this 'problem'. Sitting in waiting rooms with other women, many of whom had had the same operation and were consumed with fear, I had endless opportunities to share with them why I was not afraid. Had the hospital chaplain come in to talk to us, it is highly probable that no one would have given heed to him, feeling, 'What does he know about it?'

But they listened to me, even if only for a brief ten minutes, as I told them of the love of God in sending His Son Jesus, born the Babe at Bethlehem, to die the Man at Calvary, in order to grant us forgiveness of our sins. And they listened to me because I was one of them!

How clever God is! Just asking us to be spokes at the right time in the right place, without asking questions about the other parts of the bicycle.

For the past fifteen years I have lived, for varying periods of time, 'out of a suitcase'. I have had a lot of privileges, travelling over most of the English-speaking world, speaking at all sorts of meetings, large gatherings and small ones, to senior citizen groups and in primary school classrooms, to university students and church youth groups. On many occasions, the pace of these tours has been such that, for several weeks at a time, I have slept in a different bed almost every night. I have made thousands of acquaintances and been the recipient of an enormous amount of most generous hospitality.

But . . . how contrary can we be? I have not always welcomed this programme. I have found it to be a lonely life, never having time to get to know anyone in depth, always moving on. It was certainly tiring, always travelling and carrying suitcases from one aeroplane to another. It was frequently unrewarding, as I had no part in the follow-up work nor did I know if, as a result of a particular meeting, someone moved out towards the mission field in the subsequent years.

Once again, God had to speak to me very distinctly about my attitude. Was I not willing to be a spoke? Why was I always wanting to be the handlebars or a pedal? The responsibility was His, God's, as to where

He wanted me and what He wanted to do in and through me. He did not have to explain to me all the reasoning for His decisions. It should be sufficient for Him to give the command, and for me to jump to attention to put it into obedient action.

Was not the Lord the most lonely Man who ever walked this earth? When He was in the Garden of Gethsemane . . . when He was on trial before the Sanhedrin and before Pilate . . . when He was bound and flogged and mocked by the soldiers . . . when He walked the Via Dolorosa out to Calvary, and hung on the Cross, even 'forsaken by His Father' . . . was He not the loneliest figure imaginable? If He was willing to bear such loneliness that I might know salvation, cannot I bear a tiny portion with Him at His request?

Was not the Lord exhausted by all that took place during His earthly life – tired out by the misunderstandings of men, even of His squabbling disciples? Tired out by the strength that poured out from Him every time He ministered to the needs of others, preaching for hours on end, feeding vast multitudes, healing the sick and cleansing the leprosy sufferers? Tired out by the long night vigils in prayerful communion with His Father, to gather the strength needed for the next day's activities? If He was willing to know such weariness for me, am I not willing to be weary in His service, if that should be part of His plan for me?

Did the Lord see immediate results to His ministry? The five thousand whom He had fed, and the countless thousands whom He had healed, where were they when He hung on the Cross? 'They all forsook him and fled.' Where were His closest friends in the hour of His greatest need in the Garden of Gethsemane? Were they not asleep? 'Could you not watch with me one hour?' And the bravest of them all, His close friend, who had indeed recognised Him to be the very Son of God, the promised Messiah, and who had boasted that he would never let Him down – did he not deny all knowledge of his Lord and Master, with oaths and cursing declaring that he had never known Him? 'And the Lord turned and looked upon Peter.'

'For the joy that was set before him, he endured the cross.' He knew that the result of His suffering would be our salvation. He knew that He had won – He had finished the work that His Father had given Him to do – even if there were only a handful watching with Him round the Cross; even if it was only a dying thief who really understood and asked to be received into His kingdom.

Can I not accept to work for the *joy* of His fellowship, the privilege of being called His ambassador, His co-labourer? Why do I so hunger to see results? Why do I need to know that I am needed, that I am a 'success', when I have the certain joy of knowing that He has chosen me and sent me to bring forth much fruit?

Let me give up my selfish desire to be comfortable, or in the limelight, or personally successful, and let me learn to be content to be one of His spokes in the wheel of life. May I learn daily to seek out the right place to be His spoke, and let me pray to avoid being the wrong spoke in the wrong place at the wrong time.

Did not Paul testify to such:

> I know what it is to be in need, and I know what it is to have plenty. I have learned the secret of being content in any and every situation, whether well fed or hungry, whether living in plenty or in want. I can do everything through him who gives me strength (Phil. 4:12–13).

Truly, a humble and contented spoke, just where God had placed him!

4

The Towel:
the Practice of our Relationship
with Others

'Consider Him,' let Christ thy pattern be,
And know that He hath apprehended thee
To share His very life – His power divine,
And in the likeness of thy Lord to shine.

'Consider Him,' so shalt thou day by day
Seek out the lowliest place and therein stay,
Content to pass away, a thing of nought,
That glory to the Father's Name be brought.

Shrink not, O child of God, but fearless go
Down into death with Jesus: thou shalt know
'The power of an endless life' begin,
With 'glorious liberty' from self and sin.

'Consider Him,' and thus thy life shall be
Filled with self-sacrifice and purity;
God will work out in thee the pattern true,
And Christ's example ever keep in view.

'Consider Him.' Thy great High Priest above
Is interceding in untiring love,
And He would have thee thus 'within the veil'
By Spirit-breathed petitions to prevail.

'Consider Him,' and as you run the race,
Keep ever upward looking in His face:

And thus transformed, illumined thou shalt be,
And Christ's own image shall be seen in thee.

E. May Grimes (1868–1927)

We have now seen something of the role of the spokes
in a bicycle wheel, transmitting the power of the hub
to the outer rim in order to drive the machine forward.
We have noted that the spokes need to relate, not only
to the hub and to the rim, but also to each other, in a
correct alignment, so that the whole structure can function efficiently. This allegory seeks to point us to our need
to relate not only to God, but also to our fellow-men, if
we are to function in a way pleasing to God, in the way
for which He created us. This 'relating' to one another
can be translated as 'having fellowship' with those with
whom we come in touch in our daily lives.

We have stated that the most important relationship
in our lives is to God Himself, and we visualised this,
in Chapter Two, as the first side of a triangle, that, when
completed, will represent true *koinonia* fellowship in
the Church. Now we must look at the second side of
this triangle, which represents for us our relationship
with other people.

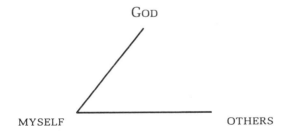

GOD

MYSELF   OTHERS

If we could picture for a moment the Lord as a Spoke
in God's plan for the world, and remember how wonderfully He always related to people around Him, this
may help us to grasp the idea as a pattern for our
own behaviour. There are so many illustrations that

we could quote: His willingness to appear needy in order to draw the Samaritan woman at the well into conversation; His sensitivity to the loneliness of the widow walking by the coffin of her only son; His availability despite His weariness to bless the children as their mothers crowded round Him; His compassion for the huge crowd, hungry at the close of a day's teaching on the mountainside; His sympathy that stretched out a hand to touch the untouchable sufferer of leprosy in order to heal him. But maybe the most startlingly clear picture is that of the Saviour tying a towel round His waist and stooping down to wash the dusty feet of His disciples.

Had He not told His disciples, 'For even the Son of Man did not come to be served, but to serve, and to give his life as a ransom for many' (Mark 10:45)?

In Chapter Two we took the yoke as the symbol of our fellowship with God. Now, we will take, as the symbol of our fellowship with others, the towel with which the Lord Jesus girded Himself when He washed His disciples' feet. The yoke was a symbol of submissive obedience and therefore of our inherent need to 'sacrifice' our self-sufficiency; the towel is a symbol of humble service and of our need to be delivered from our self-pride. Just as the yoke concealed a paradox: that in submission to Christ, we will find our greatest freedom, so the towel also conceals a paradox: that in service for Christ, we are invested with all His authority.

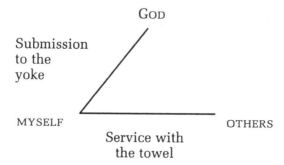

As Christians we are committed, at least in theory, to serving one another. We are all fully aware that we cannot live full, meaningful lives in total isolation from all others, and that in addition we have a responsibility, as members of the human race, to serve one another. We were created by God to live in a society.

If we are to please God and to be like our Saviour, we certainly have to agree that to live in a society, the pre-ordained requisite is that we should serve one another, without always seeking to be served.

But we need to face the question: are we honestly seeking to serve God, or are we content merely to fulfil some concept we have inherited of what Christian service means? Again, we must ask ourselves if we are seeking to serve God from the right motives, or just because we know it is right to do so – 'it is our bounden duty'? Or again, are we serving others because the very act of self-abnegation brings us some measure of self-satisfaction, knowing we have done what is right? Do I seek to serve to prove to myself or to others that I really am a Christian, in fact more Christian than some other person who does not serve as well as I do (in my biased opinion)?

In other words, can we truly say that we are serving others because we so love our Lord and Saviour that there is nothing else to do but serve? There is no other way to express the burning love in our hearts except through service to others. Has not the Lord said, 'I tell you the truth, anyone who gives you a cup of water in my name . . . will certainly not lose his reward' (Mark 9:41)? And, 'I tell you the truth, whatever you did for one of the least of these brothers of mine, you did for Me' (Matt. 25:40).

I want us to consider now the same 'whom, why, how' questions that we considered in Chapter Two when we were thinking about the yoke as the symbol of the outworking of our fellowship with God. Now we are considering the towel as the symbol of the outworking of our fellowship with others, shown in practical service in the Name of the Lord. The same three questions are pertinent:

Whom do we serve?
Why must we serve?
How shall we serve?

Whom do we serve?

We will seek to answer this question in two parts.

Though the manifestation of our service is in acts done for our fellow-men, nevertheless, first and above all else, we serve Almighty God in the same way as His Son, our Lord Jesus Christ did.

In the opening verses of John's Gospel we read:

In the beginning was the Word,
and the Word was with God, and the Word was God.
He was with God in the beginning.
Through him all things were made;
Without him nothing was made that has been made.
In him was life, and that life was the light of men.
The light shines in the darkness,
But the darkness has not understood it.

(John 1:1–5)

The title given here to our Lord Jesus Christ was 'the Word'. This in itself indicates service. Words are always our servants, conveying meaning from one being to another, be they written or spoken, read or heard. Of themselves they have no ultimate meaning, apart from the fulfilment of their purpose of communicating and passing understanding from one person to another.

Jesus came to serve His Father by revealing Him and His character through His obedience and self-expending love. There is no greater service that anyone can give to another than to reveal the character of the one served by the service rendered. 'No-one has ever seen God, but the only begotten Son, who is at the Father's side, has made him known' (John 1:18 [NIV footnote]). From eternity, the Word was and is and ever will be a Servant.

The Lord Jesus Christ was *God*, and yet He served God in creating all that was made, in giving life to all beings, and by shining light into our darkness. 'God . . . has spoken to us by his Son, whom He appointed heir of all things, and through whom he made the universe' (Heb. 1:1–2).

He came to us to 'communicate' God. Within the limitations of our humanity, He came to make the Godhead real to our human understanding. The Word was the expression of the whole Godhead in all its fullness. As such, He came to us to serve us – and we despised and rejected Him. We scorned God's Message to us, Who was the very Son of God.

Who has believed our message
  and to whom has the arm of the Lord been
    revealed? . . .
He was despised and rejected by men,
  a man of sorrows, and familiar with suffering.
Like one from whom men hide their faces
  he was despised, and we esteemed Him not

(Isa. 53:1,3)

The Word was made flesh and He became a Man, being born of a woman; and He dwelt among us, using our human form as a tabernacle, that we might see Him and come through Him to know the glory, the grace and the truth of the Godhead. 'The Word became flesh and made his dwelling among us. We have seen his glory, the glory of the One and Only Begotten, who came from the Father, full of grace and truth' (John 1:14).

Such was the birth of the Servant-King, the suffering Servant of Old Testament prophecy. And He, the Servant-Word, revealed God to us in all His glory and

majesty, His might and power – by the angel choirs who
announced His advent, by the very manner of His birth,
by the kingly gifts that welcomed His coming, by the
healing virtues that flowed from Him to the sick and
suffering throughout His life, and supremely in the
manner of His dying, when the Father, who had the
power to deliver Him from death, exerted His power
to forbear from such a deliverance that His plan for our
salvation might be fulfilled. This great Creator whom
the Servant revealed fashioned us to be His servants;
and even now He is preparing a place for us in that
very glory which He desires to reveal to us.

He, the Servant-Word, revealed God to us in all His
grace and mercy, love and forbearance, in that He veiled
His glory in the manger-birth that we might see Him; in
that He forgave our sins when we sought only physical
healing; in that He stilled the storm when our hearts
failed us for fear; and supremely in that He died for us
when we were yet His enemies, when outpoured love
became the vanquisher of the last enemy, death. This
tender Lover of our souls longs for our service, having
prepared good works for us to do from the foundation
of the world, even as He planned our redemption.

He, the Servant-Word, revealed God to us in all His
truth and holiness, purity and righteousness: through all
His teaching and ministry; through all His sinless life;
even through His wrath at the desecration of the Temple
by commercial greed; and supremely on the Cross, when
He became sin that we might become the righteousness of
God in Him, when God the Father turned away His eyes,
being of purer eyes than to behold iniquity, and when
that despairing cry was wrung from His lips, 'My God,
My God, why have you forsaken me?' (Matt. 27:46).

The Word can never be inconsistent with the Mind of
the Speaker; the Word is the expression of that Mind, as
He seeks to communicate eternal truth to us. God spoke
. . . and the Word came forth . . . and it was done. 'And
God said, "Let there be light," and there was light'
(Gen. 1:3). 'By faith we understand that the universe

was formed at God's command' (Heb 11:3), or in the Authorised Version 'by the word of God'.

God sent forth the Word to reveal, to instruct, to convict, to chasten . . . and so to serve His creatures.

> All Scripture [The WORD] is God-breathed and is useful for teaching, rebuking, correcting and training in righteousness, so that the man of God may be thoroughly equipped for every good work (2 Tim. 3:16).

And in serving us, the Word was spent. He gave 'his life as a ransom for many' (Mark 10:45).

He was always giving. When, from within the massing crowd, the woman who had been ill for many years touched Him, He knew He had been 'touched' with purpose. How did He know? He Himself tells us, 'Power has gone out from me' (Luke 8:46).

He felt divine strength going out from Him as He served this woman at the point of her need. He was always being spent on our behalf. When He had walked from Jerusalem northwards towards Galilee, and had come to Jacob's well, near to the city of Sychar, we read: 'Jesus, tired as he was from the journey, sat down by the well' (John 4:6), in order that He might meet with the lonely outcast woman who came at midday to fill her water-pots; spent that she might be satisfied. On the Cross He cried out, 'I thirst,' spent that we might be satisfied.

He who is Almighty God served from Creation to Redemption, that we, the recipients of that undeserved service, might have the privilege of serving Him.

But secondly, not only is it the Almighty Creator God who seeks our service, but it is the humble Servant Himself who calls us to be His co-labourers. In four different passages, known as 'The Servant Songs', God speaks through His servant Isaiah to reveal the future role of His Son. 'Here is my servant,' cried the Lord

God, through the prophet, 'whom I uphold, my chosen one in whom I delight' (Isa. 42:1).

God had planned the Birth, the Life and the Death of His Son from before the foundation of the world, as the only possible solution to the problem of our sin, the only way by which, whilst upholding His own holy laws, He could forgive us for breaking them (Isa. 49:1–7).

God knew that His Son would be born of a virgin (Isa. 7:14), in the town of Bethlehem (Mic. 5:2), that He would grow up, 'like a tender shoot, and like a root out of dry ground' (Isa. 53:2), chosen of His Father though despised and rejected by men. The Son declared through the writings of the prophet:

> I offered my back to those who beat me,
>   my cheeks to those who pulled out my beard;
> I did not hide my face
>   from mocking and spitting.

(Isa. 50:6)

God knew from the beginning of time that His Son must suffer – suffer humiliation at the hands of wicked men, be taken and abused, falsely accused and denied justice, flogged, scorned, spat upon – if men were to be redeemed, if men were to be reconciled to their Maker. And with a breaking heart, out of a love incomprehensible to the selfish soul of man, God planned the suffering of His Son that we might be adopted into His family as co-heirs with Christ:

> See, my servant . . .
> Surely he took up our infirmities
>   and carried our sorrows,
>   yet we considered him stricken by God,
>   smitten by him, and afflicted.
> But he was pierced for our transgressions,
>   he was crushed for our iniquities;

the punishment that brought us peace
    was upon him,
  and by his wounds we are healed.
We all, like sheep, have gone astray,
  each of us has turned to his own way;
and the Lord has laid on him
    the iniquity of us all.

(Isa. 52:13, 53:4–6)

God foresaw that His only begotten and beloved Son would be taken by cruel men, be crucified on the Cross, die and be buried, carrying away the sin of the world so that those who believe in Him might be saved and become His sons and daughters by faith.

The Word served us until He was spent:

Who, being in very nature God,
  did not consider equality with God
    something to be grasped,
but made himself nothing,
  taking the very nature of a servant,
  being made in human likeness.
And being found in appearance as a man,
  he humbled himself,
  and became obedient to death –
    even death on a cross!

(Phil. 2:6–8)

He, who was God, became man, that He might die. What exquisite humility! 'Look [– take a long earnest look at –] the Lamb of God' (John 1:29).

Such a weak timid picture, a mere lamb, and yet all history was changed by the birth of this Lamb as the Babe at Bethlehem, by the pure, sinless life He lived in Palestine, and by the cruel, savage death by crucifixion that He suffered when He died on the hill called Calvary, when the Lamb of God took away the sins of the world. Throughout the Old Testament the sacrifice of animals had been taught as the only way to approach the Holy Lord God Jehovah. The tabernacle courtyard became a place of carcasses, filled with the smell of blood and the smoke of firewood. Yet the daily repetition, even the annual great Day of Atonement, with all the hundreds of slain animals and their shed blood, could never fully atone for man's sin – there was always more. Past sacrifices could not be offered for present sins; present sacrifices could not atone for future sins. As the hymn writer expressed it:

> Not all the blood of goats,
> On Jewish altars slain,
> Could give the guilty conscience peace
> Or wash away the stain.
>
> But Christ the heavenly Lamb
> Takes all our sins away:
> A sacrifice of nobler Name
> And richer Blood than they.

> Isaac Watts (1674–1748)

Seven hundred years before the Word became man and dwelt among us, before the Lamb was slain to take away the sins of the world, the prophet Isaiah had been inspired to write one of the greatest Hebrew poems ever penned:

> He was oppressed and afflicted,
>   yet he did not open his mouth;
> He was led like a lamb to the slaughter,
>   and as a sheep before her shearers is silent,
>   so he did not open his mouth.

> (Isa. 53:7)

Amidst all the hatred and mockery of that cruel crowd in the praetorium courtyard on the first Good Friday morning; amidst all the pain of scourging and reviling in the soldiers' hall within the palace; amidst the doubt and fears and cowardly disloyalty of His closest friends, stood the spotless, sinless, sacrificial Lamb of God. He who was Almighty God became weak and defenceless for me. The Lion of Judah condescended to become the Lamb, that He might taste death in my place. In His humiliation, even justice was denied Him. Christ's whole life, from His conception by the Holy Spirit who 'overshadowed' the Virgin Mary, to His crucifixion by the pre-determinate counsel of God, was lived in total submission to His Father's will, both in service to the Godhead and also to·mankind.

Though He was indeed the very *Son of God*, He never lived for Himself. Every thought, word and action was prefaced by the concern, 'Is this My Father's will and good pleasure?' 'For I have come down from heaven not to do my will but to do the will of him who sent me' (John 6:38).

How truly He 'came down'! How low He stooped in that coming down! What a complete stripping He accepted, of all His inherent glory, that we might behold Him and be drawn to Him as He sought to reveal to us the Father! Had He kept His glory we would have been blinded, stunned, overcome by the sheer purity and abundance of brilliance. We could not have looked upon Him in our human frailty, let alone have fellowship with Him. 'I am not seeking glory for myself' (John 8:50). No! He always sought to glorify His Father. As He approached the dread hour of deepest darkness, the unfolding horror of Calvary, He cried out to His Father, 'Now my heart is troubled, and what shall I say? "Father, save me from this hour"? No, it was for this very reason I came to this hour. Father, glorify your name!' (John 12:27) And it was there on the Cross, He supremely glorified His Father, for it was there, in stark reality, that He most revealed the character of

His Father – His utter hatred and abhorrence of sin, and His unutterable, immeasurable love for the sinner. 'God ... made his light shine in our hearts to give us the light of the knowledge of the glory of God in the face of Christ' (2 Cor. 4:6).

God the Spirit does indeed shine into our hearts to lighten our darkness, and reveal to us the radiant glory of the beauty of our Lord and Saviour Jesus Christ, as by faith we see Him dying on the Cross and know it was for us:

> There was no other good enough
> To pay the price of sin:
> He only could unlock the gate
> Of heaven and let us in.
>
> We may not know, we cannot tell,
> What pains He had to bear:
> But we believe it was for us
> He hung and suffered there.
>
> Cecil Frances Alexander (1823–95)

This blessed Lamb of God, this meek and lowly Saviour, this humble Servant who was willing to be of no reputation, did He not say, 'I always do what pleases him [the Father in Heaven]' (John 8:29), and did not God reply, 'This is my Son, whom I love; with him I am well pleased' (Matt. 3:17)?

Though Son of God from all eternity, He humbled Himself, became a man, a servant, obedient, until He could cry, 'I have brought you glory on earth by completing the work you gave me to do' (John 17:4).

As *Son of Man*, He constantly submitted Himself to His Father's loving purpose – the salvation of sinners. All else had to be subordinate. It was indeed for this that His Father sent Him into the world – that we might be saved from the consequence of our sin. To redeem us from eternal death, separation from Almighty

God, the Lord Jesus Christ steadfastly set His face to go up to Jerusalem, even though He knew, without doubt, that He must 'suffer many things at the hands of the elders, chief priests and teachers of the law and . . . be killed' (Matt. 16:21).

He cried in the Garden of Gethsemane, as Son of Man, 'Not my will, but yours be done.' As we slowly and prayerfully read the accounts of the hours of agony spent there in prayer, the Spirit will reveal to us at least some insight into the innermost heart of our Saviour, in the very depth of submissive obedience.

> He withdrew about a stone's throw beyond them, knelt down and prayed, 'Father, if you are willing, take this cup from me; yet not my will, but yours be done.' An angel from heaven appeared to him and strengthened him. And being in anguish, he prayed more earnestly, and his sweat was like drops of blood falling to the ground (Luke 22:41–44).

Let us pause and ponder on those three dreadful hours on the Cross. Even nature hid her eyes as darkness covered the earth. The morbid curiosity, the stark antagonism, the resentful jealousy, the puzzled misunderstanding, the broken-hearted love, the desperate need – all emotions were stilled and silenced. His yearning prayer, breathed over that watching crowd, 'Father, forgive them, for they do not know what they are doing' (Luke 23:34), must have caused a wave of unbelief, if not of guilt, at His attitude of acceptance, so different from that usually shown by others. Then this last great cry of triumph rang out, 'It is finished,' and the Saviour, the perfected Saviour, 'bowed His head and gave up his spirit' (John 19:30).

There on the Cross, the Son of Man died an absolute death to self in every form; He demonstrated a complete submission to His heavenly Father's will and love; He finished that which was necessary for a total salvation and remission of sins and restoration into fellowship for sinners.

As our Servant, Christ exemplified submission to His Father's will. He told us so clearly that He was among us as 'one who serves' (Luke 22:27). We know that He went about 'doing good' (Acts 10:38). His whole life demonstrates to us a selflessness and self-giving for others that could only be possible as the result of submission to the Father. His self-life was completely swallowed up in His desire and compassion towards others. He had no limit to what He would give for others – time, strength, love, caring – even to the extent of having no time so much as to eat. 'We must do the work of him who sent me' (John 9:4). Always His one concern was to fulfil His Father's purpose: the foundational reason for the Word being made flesh and dwelling among men.

Many times already, we have reminded ourselves of the Scripture that the Lord 'made himself nothing, taking the very nature of a servant' (Phil. 2:7). Shortly we will turn our attention to the simple yet startling story in John's Gospel, chapter 13, where, crowded in by the world – by Judas' betrayal, by Peter's forthcoming denial, by John and James angling for personal greatness, by everyone seemingly misunderstanding Him and His Mission – 'He took a towel' and He who was indeed the Son of God, who was also the Son of Man, and beyond doubt the Servant of men, stooped down to wash our feet.

Having asked ourselves '*Who* is it that invites us to serve Him?' we have seen that it is not only the great Almighty Creator God, but also the Lamb of God who, as Son of God, obeyed His Father's commands; who, as Son of Man, went to the Cross to fulfil our redemption; who, as Servant of all, spent His life in stooping and serving.

I remember hearing a servant of God giving a Bible study on the humility of Christ, and after she had expressed many of the thoughts of this chapter, she added – surprisingly – 'But these three (the obedience to His Father's will, the going to the Cross to fulfil our redemption, and the spending of His life in stooping and serving others) do not *constitute* the humility of Christ'. I was puzzled by this apparent contradiction, until she added: 'No! they only *reflect* it!'

How true! Circumstances do not make us humble: it is how we react to them that shows whether we are humble or not. Humility is not an act of obedience to a set of circumstances but an attitude of heart revealed by the response elicited. We can be in the midst of events that give us every opportunity to express humility, but instead allow ourselves to become bitterly resentful. Christ never did that. Because of the absolute nature of His humility, and by the constancy of His communion with His Father, He was enabled to accept every circumstance as from the hand of His Father, and so triumph in it.

And this was not because, as Son of God, He could not be tempted. He was indeed no puppet, no robot; He was always fully free to choose how He would respond. He never allowed Himself to be a victim of circumstance. He was always master of His own destiny, to the extent that He had made the fulfilment of God's commands the one object of His life. Christ said, 'I lay down my life . . . of my own accord' (John 10:15,18). And again we read, 'He humbled himself' (Phil. 2:8). It is His utter humility that is His greatest strength. It was in holy dignity that He carried the Cross of shame.

We tend to think that to do certain so-called menial tasks would be 'beneath our dignity'. Or else we rise to some particular 'lowly' situation with great deliberation, and seek to 'be humble' enough to do what the task demands, as though we could then take pride in our humility! Not this way went the Crucified. And if we would be like Him, and seek to serve Him as He served both His Father and us, we have to seek the Holy Spirit to fill us with His humility.

When we look at ourselves, we see only too easily our sins and failures, our weaknesses and impotence to change ourselves, and realise how unlike we are to the Saviour. Then we long to *do* something to atone for all that is so unChristlike. But we soon discover that we have no power in ourselves to *do* anything of worth. There is nothing we can do to make ourselves more like Him. We cannot change ourselves; we cannot become what we are not by some act of willpower. It is in beholding the Lord we are changed (2 Cor. 3:18).

'Behold the Lamb of God!' For every look we take at ourselves and all our inadequacies, we need to take ten long, searching looks at Him. I long to say with Paul, 'I no longer live, but Christ lives in me' (Gal. 2:20).

We long to 'be conformed to the likeness of his Son' in all His beautiful holiness and gracious goodness and meek humility. But how? How do we find the way to become what He wants us to be, and to cease to be what we have chosen to be? 'Christ humbled himself' (Phil. 2:8). And the result of that voluntary humiliation? 'God exalted him to the highest place' (Phil. 2:9)!

As we seek to emulate that phrase 'Christ humbled himself', we need to look a little more closely at Christ's humility and how it is revealed to us.

On the one hand, throughout His life on earth we can recognise an amazing and strong personal restraint. We know that when He was reviled and falsely accused, He did not jump in to defend Himself but trusted His reputation to His Father:

> Christ suffered for you, leaving you an example, that you should follow in his steps.
>
> 'He committed no sin,
>   and no deceit was found in his mouth.'
>
> When they hurled their insults at him, he did not retaliate; when he suffered, he made no threats. Instead, he entrusted himself to him who judges justly. He himself bore our sins in his body on the tree . . . (1 Pet. 2:21–24).

He showed remarkable restraint in His dealings with His disciples when they so miserably failed to understand Him or the purpose of His mission. Even when, in righteous indignation, He overturned the tables of the money-changers in the temple courtyard, He did not display unrestrained anger in language or behaviour. He was wholly restrained on occasions when He could have justifiably demanded His rights – rights to consideration, rights to time for eating or sleeping – but instead, He always made Himself available to the needs of others.

On the other hand, He was quick to give a practical response whenever He was faced with obvious need. He did not have to be asked to cross the street to meet the need in the heart of a despairing, sorrowing widow beside the coffin of her only son. He was sensitive to the silent shame of the woman who was taken in adultery and brought before Him for judgment, compelling all the Pharisees and onlookers to depart from them so He could speak to her alone. His heart went out to His sorrowing Mother, in the anguish of her heart as He hung in agony on the Cross, commending her to the care of His beloved disciple, John. Always, always, He was sensitive to the needs of others and forgetful of His own needs.

He saw the same need that all the apostles saw when they were gathered in the Upper Room for the Passover feast. Everything had been prepared except provision for the washing of their feet before they partook of the meal. Presumably each one was debating in his mind as to who should do this menial task in the absence of a slave; each had reason to believe that it should not be himself. Jesus saw the need and unhesitatingly rose, laid aside His outer garment, twisted a towel round His waist, poured water into a basin, stooped down and began to wash their feet.

A task needed to be done, and He did it. Doubtless aware of the battle in the hearts of His disciples as to who was the least worthy, He simply stepped in and got on with the job. He was free to ignore what anyone thought of Him, or what happened to His reputation, because He knew His character was absolutely safe in the heart of His Father.

Personal restraint of lips and practical response of heart led to complete self-giving service in simple humility in the life of Christ.

For us, this humility is not to be found in aping Christ's character. It is not a cringing, vocal, meaningless claim to be humble, which mocks the very heart of the word. No! Humility comes about by the crucifixion of the self-life and the deliberate enthronement of Christ in the place of self. Only as self is crucified can I receive Christ's indwelling and be filled with all His holy, matchless humility. The fruit of the Spirit will shine through my life to the extent to which I allow God to deal with my self and to replace it with Himself.

In receiving Christ, we receive His humility: we become partakers of the divine nature. Something of the beauty of His nature enters into our innermost beings. Andrew Murray's book on humility has as its sub-title, *The Beauty of Holiness* (Lakeland, 1965). Do we long for that? Humility is an attitude of heart, that becomes more and more desirable as we gaze on the Saviour. Humility is an attitude of life that is made possible to us as we yield unreservedly to the Saviour. 'Christ in you, the hope of glory' (Col. 1:27).

How can that be? It comes about in practical experience as I submit to God. I have to learn to be submissive not just in the big and dramatic things when everyone is watching – that is not particularly difficult! – but in the little, unspectacular things as well. When God asks me to serve in the background, to be unnoticed and unthanked, to be willing to be considered a fool for His sake, how do I react? And it is not only when the world ridicules me (I should expect that), but if it is fellow-Christians (whom I feel should know better) who do the ridiculing – or even close and dear friends, who just seem unable to understand – how do I react then?

If my whole life, by His grace, is one of submission to the will of God, He will overrule my reactions so that they are honouring to Him. He will keep me close to Himself so that I am aware of His quiet, 'Well done, good and faithful servant!' But such submission requires humility of heart, a total lack of arrogance and self-importance, which can truly say, 'I have been crucified with Christ' (Gal. 2:20).

I have to seek His help and enabling, that I may be filled with a great and passionate desire to be able to say at all times, whatever the apparent cost, 'Not my will, but Thine, be done.'

> Have Thine own way, Lord, have Thine own way:
> Hold o'er my being absolute sway.
> Fashion me, mould me, after Thy will,
> While I am lying, yielded and still.

A. A. Pollard (1862–1934)

As we gaze on the Lamb of God and allow Him to empty us of our selves and fill us with Himself, Christ's humility will take over and replace our pride.

Such submission to God may be interpreted by the world as failure. There will be no loud acclaim for acts undertaken in that attitude of heart; there may be no visible fruit for service given with the one desire of glorifying the Father, rather than ourselves. 'Except a corn of wheat fall into the ground and die . . . ' (John 12:24, AV).

Is that what I want – to be ignored, forgotten, despised? Death to all that the world holds precious – acclaim, recognition, reward? Fruit only results from the death of the seed. So long as the seed hangs on to life in itself, there will be no fruit. But if it die, it will not be conscious of the fruit! Is that what I seek? Do I so long for spiritual fruit from my ministry, that I will embrace death to self that it may be achieved? 'What you sow does not come to life unless it dies' (1 Cor. 15:36).

Is the reason why there is so little new life resulting from our ministry because we are unwilling for the death of our self-life in order that the new life may be brought to birth?

Amy Carmichael records an incident early on in her missionary career in India. Rooted to the spot with anger against a fellow-missionary, she was longing to stamp her foot and retaliate with a verbal barrage when she heard a Voice say, 'See in it a chance to die.' There was to be no self-pity for being crushed, but a deliberate voluntary 'dying daily', as our Lord demonstrated throughout His earthly life.

Why must we serve?

This question, in some form or other, arises in many people's minds. The stress could be put on each of the four words in turn. Sometimes, we just long to cry out, '*Why?* Why can't I just get along quietly with my own life in my own corner? I'm not interfering with anyone else; I'm minding my own business. Why do I have to get involved with the troubles and needs of others?'

Sometimes we merely want some explanation as to why it is essential that we do become involved in other people's troubles – not because we are unwilling to be so involved, but we want to understand the *raison d'être* of the situation, 'Why *must* we serve?'

Sometimes we can see that it is necessary for someone to be involved, but simply cannot see that it is any affair of ours, 'Why must *we* serve? I've enough occupations and problems of my own, without carrying the worries of someone else as well!'

Then, lastly, there may be times we feel like saying, 'Why must we *serve?* I don't mind helping alongside others as an equal. But why use the verb "serve"? It has a connotation of the feudal system, some being over, others under, and that just doesn't appeal to me.'

Faced by the example of our Saviour's life when He was here on earth, we have to come to terms with the fact that to serve is an essential element in the most basic Christianity. 'For even the Son of Man did not come to be served, but to serve, and to give his life as a ransom for many' (Mark 10:45).

Yet the questioning persists: 'It isn't that we are unwilling to serve, but it would help if we really understood why we should!'

Firstly, then, as containers, service is essential if we are to fulfil the purpose for which we were created. We saw earlier that God created us to be containers: earthen jars to carry about the Treasure; temples to be indwelt by the Holy Spirit; branches in the Vine to bear the fruit. The purpose of our creation as containers is that we should contain, and to be functional containers demands that we serve. We are, in fact, incomplete without service.

A cup which is not filled with cool water is useless to assuage the thirst of the one who seeks to drink. It is obvious that it is not fulfilling its function while it remains empty. A house without a tenant may look attractive enough from the outside, but it cannot fulfil its function of giving protection to those under its roof while it has no inhabitant. A branch apart from the parent plant is equally useless. It must wither and die, and cannot produce fruit: it has become functionless.

Furthermore, for a container to fulfil its function, that which it contains must be spent. The act of containing alone is insufficient. A cup, though containing cool water, cannot assuage thirst until the water is drunk. The contents are spent. It is not the act of containing, but of allowing that which is contained to minister to the needs of others, that fulfils the purpose of the existence of the container.

Service completes us. Service gives meaning to our existence. By serving, we can be fulfilled: we can find our purpose in life. An exquisitely carved crystal vase may be an object of great intrinsic beauty, but if it is considered as a container, it is not fulfilling its function while it stands empty. To be filled with clean water and to carry a colourful display of flowers would fulfil its function of containing. A life lived to show off its own beauty, abilities and/or independence may attract to itself, but will not fulfil the function for which God created it. God created us to contain the Holy Spirit that He might show forth the fruit of Christianity in service to others.

Before ever we were created, God had prepared for each of us our sphere of service that we be fulfilled: 'For we are God's workmanship, created in Christ Jesus to do good works, which God prepared in advance for us to do' (Eph. 2:10).

Even though we have accepted our position as forgiven sinners, we will remain incomplete in ourselves if we do not seek out and do those 'good works' already prepared for us as our sphere of service.

Secondly, as lovers we must obey if we are to express our love, and this obedience will involve service. 'As I have served you, you must serve one another' sums up our Lord's teaching in John 13:1–17.

As we have already said, God created us in His own image that we should love as He loves – pre-eminently, we are to love Him, and then through Him to love our neighbours. 'To love and magnify God is the chief end of man,' we are taught in the Westminster Confession.

'The Lord our God, the Lord is one. Love the Lord your God with all your heart and with all your soul and with all your strength' (Deut. 6:4–5). From the time of Moses, God gave us this law, that by obedience to it we should fulfil the purpose for which we were created. If we do not love, we do not function as He intended that we should. And how do we show God our love? By obeying His commandments. God gave us the ten commandments, not only so that we might know the standard of living that is pleasing to Him, but also as a means to express the reality of our love for Him.

And with regard to our neighbours, God has commanded us to serve them as He served, thus showing that we love them as He loved.

After washing the disciples' feet, including both Peter and Judas, Jesus said to them, 'Now that I, your Lord and Teacher, have washed your feet, you also should wash one another's feet. I have set you an example that you should do as I have done for you [that is, serve one another]' (John 13:14–15).

Immediately following this, Jesus, knowing that Judas Iscariot was about to betray Him, passed the favoured morsel of bread to him. Turning to His disciples, He said, 'A new command I give you: Love one another. As I have loved you, so you must love one another' (John 13:34).

If we want to express our love for God, we shall seek to obey these two commands to their fullest extent. This will entail seeking out means to be servants. The whole life of the Lord Jesus was one of service for others as He showed us His Father's love towards us. Surely ours must emulate His if we too would fulfil His purpose for us.

Then, thirdly, service is the only way to escape self-centredness. God created us to be givers, not getters. The world says, 'What can I get out of it? Where do I come in? What gain is there for *me* if I get involved in this?' but God gives and gives and goes on giving. He is the eternal Giver. He gave His Son that we might be forgiven. 'For God so loved the world that he gave . . . ' (John 3:16).

God has shown us all through the Scriptures that giving is the tangible and real expression of love, and giving is the root of service. We are to give ourselves in service for others if we are to be Christ-like and to act in accordance with God's plan for our lives. All the time we think in terms of 'getting' – receiving esteem, being in the limelight, gaining in popularity, building up our personal reputation – we are failing to fulfil God's purpose for us, which is that we should be givers.

Oswald Chambers calls this 'The Sacrament of Sacrifice'. Commenting on the text, 'He that believeth on me, out of his belly shall flow rivers of living water' (John 7:38, AV) he says:

Jesus did not say – 'He that believeth in Me shall realise the blessing of the fulness of God,' but – 'He that believeth in Me, out of him shall escape everything he receives.' Our Lord's teaching is always *anti*-self-realisation. His purpose is not the development of a man; His purpose is to make a man exactly like Himself, and the characteristic of the Son of God is self-expenditure. If we believe in Jesus, it is not what we gain, but what He pours through us that counts. It is not that God makes us beautifully rounded grapes, but that He squeezes the sweetness out of us. Spiritually we cannot measure our life by success, but only by what God pours through us, and we cannot measure that at all.

When Mary of Bethany broke the box of precious ointment and poured it on Jesus' head, it was an act for which no one else saw any occasion; the disciples said it was a waste. But Jesus commended Mary for her extravagant act of devotion, and said that wherever His Gospel was preached 'this also that she hath done shall be spoken of for a memorial of her.' Our Lord is carried beyond Himself for joy when He sees any of us doing what Mary did, not being set on this or that economy, but being abandoned to Him. God spilt the life of His Son that the world might be saved; are we prepared to spill out our lives for Him?

'He that believeth on me, out of him shall flow rivers of living waters,' that is, hundreds of other lives will be continually refreshed. It is time now to break the life, to cease craving for satisfaction, and to spill the thing out. Our Lord is asking who of us will do it for Him?

Oswald Chambers
My Utmost for His Highest
(Marshall, Morgan & Scott, 1986)
September 2nd

When we allow our selves to become centre-stage and everything to revolve around self and what we desire for ourselves (ie. 'getters'), we fail to be what God wants us to be (ie. 'givers'). God wants His Son to be centre-stage and to have the pre-eminence, to be our King and Lord and Master, and that everything we do should please Him. 'And he is the head of the body, the church; he is the beginning and the firstborn from among the dead, so that in everything he might have the supremacy' (Col. 1:18).

The only way to escape from the tyranny of my self, (which, unhindered, will lead me into a self-imposed, imprisoned slavery) is to accept the fact that Jesus Christ must be the King and Ruler of my life, and I His 'unprofitable servant'. As I seek to be the container I was created to be, filled with the Spirit of Christ who is ready to be spent for others as the servant of all, so I will find true satisfaction and fulfilment. That is what God has purposed for me, according to the good pleasure of His will.

How shall we serve?

In the thirteenth chapter of John's Gospel, we have a picture of the *model servant*.

It was just before the Passover Feast. Jesus knew that the time had come for him to leave this world and go to the Father. Having loved his own who were in the world, he now showed them the full extent of his love.

The evening meal was being served, and the devil had already prompted Judas Iscariot, son of Simon, to betray Jesus. Jesus knew that the Father had put all things under his power, and that he had come from God and was returning to God; so he got up from the meal, took off his outer clothing, and wrapped a towel round his waist. After that, he poured water into a basin and began to wash his disciples' feet, drying them with the towel that was wrapped round him.

He came to Simon Peter, who said to him, 'Lord, are you going to wash my feet?'

Jesus replied, 'You do not realise now what I am doing, but later you will understand.'

'No,' said Peter, 'you shall never wash my feet.'

Jesus answered, 'Unless I wash you, you have no part with me.'

'Then Lord,' Simon Peter replied, 'not just my feet but my hands and my head as well!'

Jesus answered, 'A person who has had a bath needs only to wash his feet; his whole body is clean. And you are clean, though not every one of you.' For he knew who was going to betray him, and that was why he said not every one was clean.

When he had finished washing their feet, he put on his clothes and returned to his place. 'Do you understand what I have done for you?' he asked them. 'You call me "Teacher" and "Lord" and rightly so, for that is what I am. Now that I, your Lord and Teacher, have washed your feet, you also should wash one another's feet. I have set you an example that you should do as I have done for you. I tell you the truth, no servant is greater than his master, nor is a messenger greater than the one who sent him. Now that you know these things, you will be blessed if you do them' (John 13:1–17).

This passage gives a beautiful picture of the whole life-ministry of Jesus Christ. In the Upper Room, that evening nearly 2,000 years ago, He rose from supper; so, in heaven's glory, He had risen from His Father's side. Here we read that He laid aside His outer garment;

there He laid aside the very glory of the Godhead. He wrapped a towel round Him in this story; there, He clothed Himself with human flesh. Here, He poured water into a basin; there, He poured forth His blood on the cross of Calvary. In the Upper Room, we read that He took again His outer garment, just as He received again His body in the Resurrection; and He sat down, as now He is sitting down by His Father in glory.

Just as throughout His earthly life, so here in this simple story, Christ highlights for us various aspects of real, godly service.

Firstly, let us note the extent of the love of Jesus for His disciples.

The final events in Christ's human life were about to take place. It was the last evening before the trial scene, the scourging and the crucifixion. As He had done each of the three previous years, Jesus was spending this evening with His friends, 'keeping the Passover Feast'. In His heart was the knowledge of the morrow and of all the horror of suffering that awaited Him, that the very purpose of His birth and life might be fulfilled. In His prayer that night in the Upper Room, He cried aloud to His Father, 'I have brought you glory on earth by completing the work you gave me to do!' (John 17:4).

We read that Jesus, 'Having loved his own who were in the world . . . now showed them the full extent of his love' or as the Authorised Version translates it, 'he loved them to the end' (John 13:1).

That is a deeply moving statement. It underlines the utter consistency and steadfastness of the deep love of God for us, His children by adoption. He has kept on giving and serving and loving us right to the end. Was He thinking of 'the end' of His own earthly life? Or was this referring to 'the end' of our sin, reminding us that there are no depths to which His love cannot reach, no sin that He cannot forgive? Or was He referring to 'the end', the furthest possible imaginable limit of the bounds of love itself?

If we compare our love and service for others with this standard, how do we fare? How easily we give up halfway! How easily are we discouraged by seeing no obvious results or by adverse conditions? How easily do we grumble at the time involved or at the apparent sacrifice of what we think of as our personal liberties? How hard do we find it to forgive in the way He forgives us, so that we really cannot love the person who has wronged or offended us? How much do we demand of the other person in return for our love and our service, in a way that Christ has never demanded of us?

Had Christ demanded reparation, or restitution, or even an apology for sins committed against Him would any of us ever have been saved? Isn't the most shattering aspect of His love that 'While we were still sinners, Christ died for us' (Rom. 5:8)? Do we really love and serve others 'to the end' of all our resources, without setting limits, without preconditions?

We have to will to give instead of to get, to serve instead of to be served, to love when it would be less costly to be disinterested.

> Make me a channel of Your peace.
> Where there is hatred let me bring Your love;
> Where there is injury, Your pardon, Lord;
> And where there's doubt, true faith in You.
>
> > Oh, Master, grant that I may never seek
> > So much to be consoled as to console;
> > To be understood as to understand;
> > To be loved, as to love with all my soul.
>
> Make me a channel of Your peace.
> Where there's despair in life, let me bring hope;
> Where there is darkness, only light;
> And where there's sadness, ever joy.
>
> Make me a channel of Your peace.
> It is in pardoning that we are pardoned,

In giving to all men that we receive;
And in dying that we're born to eternal life.

(From the prayer of St Francis of Assisi)

We have to will to keep on loving even when we don't
feel like it. True love has little to do with our emotions
or our feelings. It is a fact that has to be demonstrated
in service, whether we feel like it or not. Once our will
is broken, so far as self-willed effort is concerned, then
we can be yoked to Christ. Once we are so yoked, and
have accepted His right to be the will that drives the
team, then we can love, and so serve, with His persis-
tence 'to the end'. Are we ever weary in well-doing?
We can thank God for His unending and undemand-
ing love towards ourselves, and that Jesus Christ was
never weary in well-doing on our behalf: He never gave
up!

Secondly, in verse 3 we read that Jesus served His
disciples by washing their dusty, smelly feet, knowing
that 'the Father had put all things under His power, and
that He had come from God and was returning to God.'
Jesus had nothing to prove, and so He was free to serve.
He knew where He stood in His Father's estimation: His
character was secure in heaven, however maligned on
earth.

We are so often seeking to prove something to ourselves or to others. This can become such a preoccu-
pation that we are no longer free to serve. It may be a
need to impress people with one's seniority or abilities
(often because of an underlying insecurity and uncer-
tainty). It may be a private agenda, which one is so
determined to see through to completion that one is
blinded to the needs of others. Perhaps it is just an
unresolved hunger on my own part to be accepted by
people for who and what I am, to be recognised and
appreciated; or an unwillingness to be trampled on,
manipulated, ignored or made use of.

Am I so busy trying to prove to myself that I am all that I claim to be and that I can do all that is expected of me, that I dare not take on a piece of service that is outside my prescribed professional task, something that is not mentioned in my job description, for fear that I might fail? Am I tempted to refuse to accept the extra responsibility asked of me, because the time involved might jeopardise my chances of promotion? Any or all of these attitudes can make me unwilling to go the extra mile or take on the extra task in some service for which I know instinctively that I won't be thanked.

If any of these emotions are fighting in the background of my mind, I cannot be free to give truly Christ-like service. Jesus Christ had nothing to prove and no secret agenda. He knew His Father, and He knew that His Father knew Him. He knew that He was in the centre of His Father's will. He knew that His Father was willing to enable Him to complete the task that had been assigned to Him. This was His security. He was not worried by what men thought of Him because He knew that His Father knew the truth.

Someone has rightly said, 'Reputation is what men think of us, and really is of no account. Character is what God knows of us, and is of infinite value and counts for eternity.'

Because the Lord Jesus Christ was rightly related to His Father, He could relate to people around Him without difficulty. That must surely be the secret for us. To be in fellowship with my neighbours is to be rightly related to them, and that flows from a right relationship to God Himself. The yoke must come before the towel.

Then again, Jesus was never too busy for people. When mothers brought their children to Him that He might bless them, even though He had had a hectic day, He not only had time for them, but He actually made them feel welcome. When the woman touched Him in the pressing throng of the crowd, He not only healed her but He also had time to stop and search her out, speaking words of comfort to her personally, as though she was the only person in His world just then.

On one occasion when Jesus was being entertained to dinner in the home of a Pharisee, 'a woman who had lived a sinful life' came in. 'As she stood behind him at his feet weeping, she began to wet his feet with her tears. Then she wiped them with her hair, kissed them and poured perfume on them' (Luke 7:37–8). Jesus did not rebuke her roughly, bidding her go away and come to Him at a more convenient time. He was not embarrassed by her show of affection, nor by the fact that He was in someone else's home. He had time for her and a willingness to accept publicly her ministrations, even though the Pharisee thought that He should have been concerned that she was a sinner. It did not matter to Jesus what the Pharisee thought at that moment. He was able to put Himself in the woman's place and understand her need to express her love by the only means at her disposal.

At that moment, Jesus was not concerned with proving His ability to discern and judge, although in fact He had discerned and correctly judged the woman's heart, and also the Pharisee's heart! Jesus could rest in the assurance that God knew the truth, both about Himself and also about the woman. When I find I cannot forgive someone for a slight or a cruel action or for what appears to be the deliberate spreading of false rumours, can I not rest in the quiet assurance that God knows the truth? Why do I have to prove my innocence before I can continue to offer loving service? Did not Paul write to the Romans:

Do not take revenge, my friends, but leave room for God's wrath, for it is written: 'It is mine to avenge; I will repay,' says the Lord [Deut. 32: 35]. On the contrary:

If your enemy is hungry, feed him;
    if he is thirsty, give him something to drink.

In doing this, you will heap burning
                    coals on his head [Prov. 25:21–2].

Do not be overcome by evil, but overcome evil
with good (Rom. 12:19–21).

When Jesus entered the Temple courtyard and saw
the tradesmen with their cattle, sheep and doves, and
the money-changers with their Temple coinage and
balances, He was incensed at the way they were cheating the country folk who arrived for the annual festi-
val. They were overcharging them for the animals they
bought for sacrifice, and they were undervaluing their
currency as they gave them Temple coinage in exchange
for their country money. Jesus was indignant to see the
place filled with noise and shouting like a busy stock
exchange, instead of being still with a sense of awe at
the presence of Almighty God.

'So He made a whip out of cords, and drove all from
the temple area, both sheep and cattle; he scattered
the coins of the money-changers and overturned their
tables' (John 2:15–16), oblivious of the stir that this
would cause, and the hatred that would be unleashed
against Him by the Pharisees and Scribes and Temple
authorities. All that mattered to Him was His Father's
honour; whatever they thought of Him was of no
importance.

Jesus never had a bodyguard to protect Him from
interruptions. Most of us feel we could cope with our
lives and remain unruffled, if only we didn't have to
cope with distractions. In fact, the higher up the social
ladder we succeed in climbing, the more we are able to
surround ourselves with an effective bodyguard. How
many times does it happen that someone tries to ring
up their local General Practitioner when a member of
the family falls ill, only to be answered by the recep-
tionist who absolutely refuses to put the call through
to her boss. She is prepared, grudgingly, to make us an
appointment for four days hence, but is hard-hearted

towards our plea for immediate help. I remember an occasion of desperate urgency in Zaire, when it was essential (as I saw the situation) that I should see the British Ambassador immediately. I had to work my way past an aggressive doorman, a junior secretary, an underling representing the consul, a vice-consul, before I even reached the Ambassador's private secretary's office. I never did reach the Ambassador himself! We like our bodyguards. They make it possible for us to get on with our work undisturbed by interruptions.

There was never a barrier between Jesus and His people. He was always willing for interruptions: He almost seemed to welcome them! Having crossed the Sea of Galilee to have a quiet day with His disciples, apart from the constant pressure of the crowds, He 'saw a large crowd' who had foot-slogged all through the night, right round the lake, in order to hear more of His teaching. Immediately, with no thought of His own weariness or plan for the day, we read that, 'He had compassion on them, because they were like sheep without a shepherd' (Mark 6:34). He gave up His right to a day of peace and quiet, for rest and personal refreshment, and 'began teaching them many things'. As the day passed and evening approached, He went the second mile and provided them all with physical sustenance before sending them homewards! It was a severe interruption to His own desired programme, but He behaved in such a way, that 5,000 people felt welcomed and wanted.

Having already 'made himself of no reputation' (Phil. 2:7 AV), Jesus had no reputation to guard and keep. He had no appearance to maintain, because it did not matter to Him what people thought of Him, so long as He knew He was doing that which pleased His Father. He had no status to which people had to bow down, and therefore He was able to serve all and sundry, continuously and indiscriminately.

Am I free to pick up the towel and do the insignificant, for the love of Jesus, with no hidden motives? Can

I be free from worrying about what people will think of me, and whether my action could be interpreted as being demeaning to my position? Oswald Chambers said, 'Can I use a towel as He did? Towels and dishes and sandals, all the ordinary sordid things of our lives, reveal more quickly than anything what we are made of. It takes God Almighty Incarnate in us to do the meanest duty as it ought to be done.'

Thirdly, Jesus did not 'pick and choose' whom He would serve. He did not have favourites, nor were there some whom He refused to serve. That Maundy Thursday in the Upper Room, when He worked His way around the circle of disciples, washing their feet, He did not pass by Judas – and yet He knew that within the hour Judas would betray Him to the religious rulers. Jesus knew Judas was a traitor, yet He treated him with the same loving concern as the rest.

Would I have done that? I hardly think so! In fact, some might reply 'No way!' We are not usually very willing to serve anyone who can give us nothing in return, let alone someone who is intent on doing us harm. We often refuse to serve someone who has wronged us or hurt us until we are satisfied, not only that they have confessed their wrong and asked our forgiveness, but also that they have made clear and public restitution, however costly and humiliating that may be. Our service, as an expression of love and appreciation of another person, is so dependent on how we feel about them. It is rarely dispassionate: or indifferent to applause and reward. It is frequently part of a bargaining mechanism, giving in like measure as I receive. How deeply grateful we have to be to God that that is not how He has treated us!

Then, too, Jesus washed Judas' feet, realising that only He knew what was in the heart of Judas and what he was about to do. Therefore He didn't do it in order that they might all think how wonderful He was to be so generous and forgiving in spirit. Jesus' service to Judas was just the same as He was rendering to the rest. Some of us have to be seen to be serving before we'll serve. We need the applause of people, saying how gracious or generous or public-spirited we are, before we'll act. We want people to know who it was that did the service, even if they did not actually see it being done, so that we do not lose the praise. Jesus worked even when there was no praise.

Some of us are willing to serve those whom we think of as 'big and important', but are unwilling to serve those we consider our equals on the social ladder, let alone those 'beneath us'. It sounds good to have been asked to wash the boss's car, but not the doorkeeper's. It sounds humble, perhaps, to wash the feet of leprous sufferers on the mission field, but not very spectacular to do a small service for a fellow-missionary. Jesus Christ served everyone equally, with no reference to their place on the ladder of public opinion.

When Jesus stooped to wash His disciples' feet He took the position of the lowliest slave on the totem pole of the day. Who else would have done it? Did not even the Rabbis refuse to allow their students to do that for them, though they did all sorts of other services? No, only a slave could be allowed to wash feet! And now at the Passover Feast, were not all the disciples silently arguing in their hearts that it was beneath them and someone else ought to offer to do the task? When jobs are being handed out, who offers to go and buy the tea, milk and sugar, and stand in the supermarket queue to pay the bill? Even pouring and taking round the cups of tea is preferable to that: at least you would then be seen to be serving!

Indians have a proverb: 'Do you have to wake a sleeping beggar to give him a coin?'

Jesus stooped down to wash their feet – right down. He came down from heaven's glory, humbled Himself, and obeyed unto death, even the death of the Cross. But God raised Him up and highly exalted Him, giving Him a Name that is above every name.

Fourthly, Jesus exposed pride in the heart of man as the poison that makes it impossible to serve with true humility and grace. On the one hand, He gave His disciples an example of true humility in action – the ability to serve all and sundry graciously, without looking over one's shoulder for praise and acknowledgment, without getting weary in well-doing, even when there was no advantage to oneself.

And on the other hand, He revealed the need for inner cleansing from daily contact with sin. Before the disciples had set out on their walk to come to the Upper Room for the feast, they had doubtless bathed all their body. So it was only their feet, dusty from the road, that needed washing on arrival. Likewise, we were cleansed from our burden of sin when we first came to the Saviour in repentance, receiving His free gift of salvation. But now on our daily journey through this sinful world, our 'feet' get contaminated and need regular washing. We cannot help seeing posters and graffiti which dirty our eyes and minds; we cannot help hearing the rough language around us, when the Name of our God is taken in vain; and so we need our 'feet' washed daily.

But it is not only these externals that cause contamination and the need for daily cleansing. Jesus' encounter with Peter highlighted the pride that lay deep within the inner recesses of his heart, which also urgently needed cleansing away. When He knelt at Peter's feet, Peter exclaimed, 'You, Lord, wash my feet?' It sounded humble enough, but Jesus saw through the deception and discerned what was probably going on in Peter's heart.

'You can't understand Me now,' Jesus replied, 'but you will later.' Jesus was teaching him an inner lesson, as well as the obvious outer one, but Peter was in no state to learn either!

'Never!' he exclaimed with one breath: and then did a U-turn, and almost in the same breath, cried, 'OK, Lord, but please do it my way. Not just like You have done it for all the others, Lord, but wash *all* of me!' Was he being even more humble, or was this actually inverted pride?

Ever since Peter had made that great declaration: 'You are the Christ, the Son of the Living God!' Jesus had been teaching His disciples that He must suffer:

> From that time on Jesus began to explain to his disciples that he must go to Jerusalem, and suffer many things at the hands of the elders, chief priests and teachers of the law, and that he must be killed and on the third day be raised to life (Matt. 16:21).

Was Peter beginning to register the import of those words? If Jesus was to be crucified, then one of the band of twelve would have to take over the leadership, and who was better suited and trained than he, Peter? Had he not been singled out by Christ for special treatment? He was one of the very first to join the band of disciples. He had been there with the Master at the raising of Jairus' daughter. He had been there with Him on the Mount of Transfiguration. Yes, undoubtedly He would make the best leader when the day came: he was indeed what some would have called 'a born leader'.

But his concept of leadership was offended by Christ's act of foot-washing. If he, Peter, was to become the leader, he had no intention of washing their feet! In fact, if the truth were told, one reason that he wanted to become the leader was that he might *avoid* such menial tasks. Jesus was making a mockery of leadership. He was getting everything upside down, topsy-turvy.

'No, Peter,' Jesus remonstrated with him, 'if you don't let Me wash you from that inner core of pride, because of which you want to be the greatest, there is no way that you can serve Me. You cannot serve with pride: you would just choose whom you'd serve and when. Let Me cleanse you from that inner poison of pride, washing your motives and attitudes, then you can serve Me and others as I have served you.'

And it wasn't only Peter. Even on their way to Jerusalem for the Passover Feast, had not the others been discussing, who would be the greatest among them? John and James had persuaded their Mother to speak on their behalf, asking for the best seats in heaven – so little did they understand all that Jesus was teaching and demonstrating to them. Had He not taught them, 'Whoever wants to become great among you must be your servant, and whoever wants to be first must be slave of all' (Mark 10:43–4)? All of them were filled with carnal pride, which showed so obviously in the fact that none of them was willing to take the towel and the basin and wash the feet of the assembled party.

I expect we all know the illustrative story from China of the magnificent stately Bamboo, with its great head of fine fronds. The King had a job that needed doing, and he saw that the stately Bamboo could do it well.

'I want to use you today,' the King said, looking up at Bamboo's magnificent head of waving plumes.

'How wonderful!' thought the proud Bamboo, 'that is just what I have been waiting for.'

'But to use you, I will have to cut you down,' the King said.

'All right,' conceded Bamboo, 'so long as you use me.'

'I must strip you of all your natural glory,' the King confided to him.

Bamboo thought about it. To lose his head of fronds of which he was so inordinately proud seemed a big price to pay, yet . . . he really did long to be used by the King. 'Yes, King, if that is the only way,' he said at last, 'so long as I am used.'

'I must split you in two all down your length, and scour out your heart, breaking down all the partitions,' the King whispered to him.

'O King, whatever the cost – yes, I *must* be used!' Bamboo eventually cried.

So he was cut down, all the fronds stripped away from him; he was split in two down his whole length and all his heart scoured out of him. Then, with nothing left of his original natural beauty, the two lengths were laid end to end, and water from the King's spring was fed down to the rice fields in the valley below.

Am I willing for such treatment 'if only I am used'? Do I agree to be 'cut down to size', to lose all that I think of as my natural assets (as Paul did, who saw that all such were but rubbish if he might win Christ (Phil. 3:7–11)), to be split in two, my heart laid bare to all the insults and hurts that may well be hurled at me, scoured of all that blocks the free flow of the Spirit, and so used as a channel to carry the Spirit to the needy all around me?

> Channels only, blessed Master,
> But with all Thy wondrous power
> Flowing through us, Thou canst use us
> Every day and every hour.

Mary E. Maxwell

Can I cry out of the depths of my heart, 'Yes, Lord, anything, so long as You can use me to the furtherance of Your purposes'?

'Girt with the towel' to serve, in utter Christ-like humility – is that a picture of my service and yours – both for God Almighty and also for my fellow-men? Is that my understanding of what it means to have fellowship, both with God and with one another? Am I living in such close relationship to God and to my fellow-men, that I long to serve them as an expression of my love for them and therefore of my fellowship with them in their daily lives?

PART III

GOD'S INVITATION TO SHARE IN THE FELLOWSHIP OF HIS SUFFERINGS

5

God's Relationship with Others: the Rim

We come now to the third part of our analogy, drawn from the bicycle wheel.

In our first chapter, the need for the hub to be in place if a wheel is to be of any practical use portrayed for us the absolute necessity of a living relationship between God and ourselves. Jesus Christ must be central in our hearts and lives if we are to enjoy true spiritual fellowship with the Father, the Son and the Holy Spirit, and so to function in the way for which God created us.

Secondly, the spokes of the wheel helped us to understand that the relationship between God and ourselves will be revealed in our everyday lives by an attitude of servanthood to those around us, which, I contend, is fundamental to any enjoyment of true fellowship with our fellow-men. Each spoke alone is useless and weak: but spokes working together in harmony give strength to and maintain the shape of the wheel. As each Christian seeks to serve those around him, so relationships will be built up that lead into a truly godly fellowship, and the Church will then function in the way for which it was created.

Now we come to the third and deepest area of relationships and so of true fellowship. In our picture language, this is the essential relationship of the hub to the whole rim. The spokes are needed to transfer the power from the one to the other and so to drive the bicycle forward, but are of themselves relatively unimportant. However, the job could not be achieved without them: and so in the spiritual realm, the Omnipotent Sovereign Lord God has chosen to need our cooperation as He reaches out to the needy world around us. The big question is, Are we willing to enter in to the 'fellowship of His sufferings'?

We each have our own bit of 'world' to which we can personally relate, our own section of 'rim' to which our spoke is attached. For many this will be the immediate family; the colleagues at the place of work; those people met in shops, schools, hospitals and church in daily life, be it in the homeland or in some foreign land where missionaries and others have chosen to live and work.

But we are well aware that our small bit of rim is only part of the whole. The world is too vast for us to relate individually to more than a very small section, but we know that God relates to the whole; just as the hub has to relate to the whole rim, and not just the section to which any one spoke is attached. God invites us to be sharers in His relationship to the whole universe of mankind.

The main points to grasp from our analogy are the apparent unimportance of the individual spokes, the essential need for all the spokes to work together, and the overwhelming desire of the hub to transfer its power to the rim via the spokes. How willing am I to see myself in the light of such a parable? Do I firmly believe that, 'Apart from me you can do nothing' (John 15:5)?

It is not natural for human beings readily to accept that they are useless in the fulfilment of a particular function without the help and assistance of another. Yet spiritually, that is what God is saying to us. Without a vital and active relationship with God, we can of ourselves do nothing to promote God's interests in the world.

In the execution of His programme for the world, Almighty God has chosen to limit Himself to the employment of ambassadors. It is obvious that God could have achieved His goals for mankind without our help; but He has chosen to make use of us as His representatives and as His mouthpieces.

The band of twelve apostles were chosen and trained to be the first missionaries to take the Gospel to the then-known world after the Day of Pentecost. Is it possible that the Lord had moments of doubt as to the feasibility of this plan? Did He look at that weak group of argumentative and vacillating men, and wonder if His Father's plan could ever succeed? Could such vital and delicate work really be entrusted to such untrustworthy agents? In Luke chapter 14, verses 25 to 33, we can almost hear the Lord deliberating, and coming to the conclusion, 'Yes, *if*...' and then stating the three essentials if the job was to be done:

> If anyone comes to me and does not hate his father and mother, his wife and children, his brothers and sisters – yes, even his own life – he cannot be my disciple. And anyone who [does not deny himself, and who] does not carry his cross and follow me cannot be my disciple ... Any of you who does not give up everything he has cannot be my disciple (Luke 14:26–7,33).

A disciple has to so love Jesus as Lord and Master, that any affection he has for himself will seem like hatred by comparison. His love for Christ must make everything else pale into insignificance. It must be so vital and real that he would honestly lay down his life for his Saviour rather than deny or fail Him. Paul, after listing out all his earthly credentials and natural assets, says:

> But whatever was to my profit I now consider loss for the sake of Christ. What is more, I consider everything a loss compared to the surpassing greatness of knowing Christ Jesus my Lord, for whose sake I have lost all things. I consider them rubbish, that I may gain Christ and be found in him, not

having a righteousness of my own that comes from
the law, but that which is through faith in Christ –
the righteousness that comes from God and is by
faith. I want to know Christ and the power of his
resurrection and the fellowship of sharing in his
sufferings, becoming like him in his death (Phil.
3:7–10).

If I want to be usable by the Master as His ambassador
in the world, Jesus tells me that I must deny my rights
to myself. I have to learn to cease thinking about myself,
how things affect *me*, and how people relate to *me*; and
think instead of how to please God, how situations
affect Him, what people are thinking of Him and how
I can help them to come into a proper relationship
with Him. In other words, I have to act like a spoke!
I have to realise that my only importance in the wheel
is transferring the power of the Hub to the rim.

When God sees children suffering and dying of star-
vation in a world where there is ample food for all to
eat adequately, His heart must be torn with grief. Can
that grief flow through my spoke? When He sees cruelty
and brutality in wars where He had planned peace and
kindness, His heart must be burdened with distress. Can
that distress flow through my spoke? When the sin of
mankind weighs upon His heart as in the agony in the
Garden of Gethsemane, am I watching with Him – or
am I asleep? Can that agony flow through my spoke?

Do I truly and earnestly desire to be in such close
relationship with God that I am willing to deny myself,
take up my cross and follow Him, even though this
leads to Calvary? As a spoke, do I see it as my greatest
privilege that I can link the power of the Hub to the need
of the rim, without wasting energy worrying about the
intrinsic value (or lack of such) of the spoke itself? Does
it matter to me that others should recognise my part in
the plan, or am I so in tune with the Divine Heart of
God that all I long for is the fulfilment of His plan?

Pause for a moment, try to picture a bicycle in your

mind's eye and watch it as it gathers speed – can you see the spokes? You will soon discover the answer is 'No!' You can still see the hub and the rim, but the spokes all melt into each other in a hazy blur: they are no longer visible as separate identities.

We hardly need to be reminded that the rim cannot turn and carry the bicycle forward on its own: it is dependent on the power from the revolving hub to be transmitted through the spokes to enable its progress. The spokes are essential in this process, yet they are practically invisible when the bicycle gathers speed. But even when invisible, we know they are still there!

When we, as Christians, are 'complete in the Lord Jesus Christ', others around us will be able to see, hear and sense Him through us, even if they do not notice or remember us. It is essential that we are not such strong personalities that we block their view of the Master. If we would serve them, it must be as pointers to the Saviour, 'Let your light shine before men, that they may see your good deeds and praise your Father in heaven' (Matt. 5:16). Those around us are not meant to be drawn to us to glorify ourselves and so to increase our ego, but to be drawn to our Saviour and to glorify our heavenly Father. It should be for us as it was for John the Baptist, 'He [the Lord Jesus Christ] must become greater; I must become less' (John 3:30).

We are to be mirrors, correctly angled so that anyone looking into us will see the perfect reflection of the Saviour. The surface of our mirror must be spotlessly clean so that nothing can mar that reflection. No one is normally interested in seeing a mirror, but only the image reflected in it. Am I willing to go unnoticed, forgotten, even unthanked, so long as others see the Lord reflected in me? Is my one longing that they should relate to Him, with no thought of myself?

A number of years ago I was invited to speak at a Christian Ladies' Dinner Club at Dunblane, in Central Scotland. During my address I told three or four stories from my experience in Africa, to illustrate the great love of God and His compassionate care for all who put their trust in Him. The first of these stories is now well-known to many of you. It told of how God provided us with a hot-water bottle for a premature baby whose Mother had died in childbirth. Four years later I was again invited to Dunblane, to meet with the same group of ladies, though the group had now grown to almost three times its original size. During the course of the evening I asked how many had been there four years before. All around the restaurant ladies put their hands up, and I was encouraged.

'Please keep your hands up for a minute,' I requested. 'I want to ask you a question.'

Many looked slightly uncomfortable, perhaps wishing they had not been so quick to identify themselves! All the newcomers looked at them and wondered, 'What next?'

'May I ask if any of you can remember the first story I told you last time I was here?' – possibly an unkind question when one realises that they had had many and varied speakers at their monthly gatherings over those four intervening years! Slowly one or two began to respond.

'It was about a dolly,' one ventured.

'Yes,' interjected another, 'and a hot-water bottle!'

A third one butted in: 'And a ten-year-old who prayed!'

'And the parcel came.' Several joined in together as their memories had been jogged and the story began to come back to them.

Needless to say, I was delighted that so many had remembered the story so well, but then I posed another question, asking the newcomers to take careful note as to who was able to answer me.

'Who remembers who sent the parcel?'

And there was silence – complete silence.

'That wasn't very fair of me, was it?' I confessed to the somewhat embarrassed guests. 'But that was just the response I wanted!'

For any of you who do not know the story, let me briefly fill you in with some details. I had been called to the maternity wing of our hospital at Nebobongo, in the north-eastern corner of Zaire. Sadly, despite all I sought to do that night, the mother died and I was left to care for a tiny premature baby. The pupil midwives left the delivery room, each with a task to perform. Shortly, one came back with a woeful face.

'I'm so sorry, doctor,' she began. 'I boiled the kettle, and was filling the hot-water bottle, when it burst! And it is our last hot-water bottle,' she added ruefully.

There was no good being over-upset: hot-water bottles do not grow on trees, and we had no chemist shops down the forest pathways where we could buy a new one.

'Wrap the baby up carefully,' I told the others as we oiled the little body and laid it in the cot. 'Now put the cot as near the fire as is safely possible. One of you must sit between the baby and the doorway, to keep it free from draughts, and to see it remains warmly wrapped up. If the baby gets cold, it will die.'

Next day, I had gone over to the children's home to have prayers with the young people. Amongst other topics, I told them of the little baby and of its two-year-old sister who was crying because her mother had died. I mentioned the burst hot-water bottle, and asked the children to pray for the midwives who were caring for the baby, that God would help them to stay awake through the night, to see that the baby did not get cold. During the prayer time, one little ten-year-old girl, Ruth, prayed in the very blunt way of our African children.

'Please, God, send us a hot-water bottle. And God, it will be no good tomorrow, the baby will be dead. So please send it this afternoon.' While I gasped at the simple audacity of the prayer, she added, 'And would You please also send a dolly for the little girl so she'll know You really love her?'

I confess I did not say 'Amen'. In my heart of hearts, I did not think it was possible, not even for our Almighty God.

That afternoon, a truck drove into our village and delivered a large parcel, leaving it on the verandah of my home. When I arrived, I saw my name, English stamps, a London postmark, and Mrs Betty Ponsford's address in Bromley, Kent. It was the first parcel I had ever received since going to Africa. I felt a lump in my throat. All of a sudden, I felt scared to open it. Had God really heard and answered that child's prayer?

I gathered the children round me and we opened it together. Carefully undoing every knot in the string, unfolding each layer of paper, prising off the Sellotape ... I drew out several brightly coloured jerseys that the children loved; knitted bandages for the leprosy patients, so invaluable in those days for the awful ulcers on their poor feet; some soap; a box of mixed dried fruit; and then ... from the middle of the parcel, a brand new Boots' rubber hot-water bottle!

I cried. I had not asked God for it. I had not honestly believed God could do it.

Ruth was in the front line of children. She rushed forward, exclaiming, 'If God has sent the hot-water bottle, He must have sent the dolly!'

She dived into the parcel with both hands, and from the depths she pulled out the dolly!

'Can I go over with you, Mummy, to give the dolly to that little girl, so she'll know that Jesus really loves her?' Ruth had never doubted, and God had wonderfully honoured her child-like trust in Him.

That parcel had been on the way for five whole months: and before that, through a whole school year, the girls of the intermediate section of the Girl Crusaders' Union, Bromley Class, had been knitting those jerseys and bandages. When Betty had packed up the parcel, she had heard God prompting her to put in that hot-water bottle, even though she must have questioned the reason for it, knowing that I lived on the equator! And one of the younger girls of the class had asked to put her dolly in for an African child.

No wonder that, even four years later, many at

the Dunblane Ladies' Meeting had remembered the story, and were able to recall the hot-water bottle, the dolly, the praying child, the parcel – but was it really surprising that *no one* could recall the name of the person who packed the parcel, nor where she lived?

You could say that the name or address of the sender really didn't matter.

And yet, of course, it mattered tremendously! If Betty hadn't been there to encourage the girls in her class to do the knitting, to pack the parcel, to include the hot-water bottle and the dolly and to pay the price of the stamps, the story would never have occurred. Betty's name and the name of the class may not appear to be very important in the telling of the story – they can be forgotten without the story losing anything of its poignancy. And even if they had never been thanked, that also would not have changed the facts of the story.

Once the bicycle wheel is moving, the spokes are no longer individually seen – but they have to be there! Without the spokes, the bicycle would not move at all.

Even should we forget the names of the donors, even should we fail to thank them, they are known to God, and He does not forget them. They are essential to Him in the fulfilment of His purpose: in this case to provide the material need of that tiny, unnamed baby in a small unknown hospital in the vast forest hinterland of Zaire. So concerned was God for that baby's welfare, that He had prompted that group of schoolgirls in south-east England to begin their knitting for the parcel before the baby had even been conceived! Truly:

'For my thoughts are not your thoughts,
    neither are your ways my ways,'
        declares the Lord.
'As the heavens are higher than the earth,
    so are my ways higher than your ways
    and my thoughts than your thoughts.'

(Isa. 55:8–9)

One could share so many stories where people have acted as spokes, bringing the love and power of God to meet a specific need. Each story illustrates not only that the spoke is essential to channel the power of the Hub to that particular bit of the rim, but also that the purpose can be achieved without the spoke being individually noticed, thanked and remembered.

I remember when God first challenged me to start work amongst leprosy patients. It was barely one year after my arrival on the mission field. We were busy building the first wards for our new hospital. I was working virtually single-handedly at that time, with seven national students whom I was seeking to train as ward orderlies. The workload was heavy and the responsibility pretty frightening. Time off was unknown: there was no one else to go on duty! Every hour of every day (and often of nights as well) was full. And now came the demand to start yet another clinic!

It would mean building a separate room and buying separate stores and equipment, as the feeling in those days was strongly opposed to treating the 'dread disease of leprosy' among other patients in a general clinic. I had neither time nor money for such an undertaking, and was irritated to be goaded into doing so. But I could not escape the clear direction from God that this was what He wanted me to do.

Unwillingly I sent off for the needed drugs and syringes, bandages and basic equipment. Grudgingly we began to erect a small house behind my home to act as a leprosy clinic. Several weeks later, a passing lorry-driver brought me a carton of supplies from the distant city of Kisangani. Helped by Aunzo, my first leprosy patient, I unpacked the ordered supplies, and drew out the accompanying invoice. The total was 4,320 Belgian Congo francs. It seemed a phenomenal sum at that time, equalling nearly three months' allowance! I certainly did not have that sort of money available to pay the bill.

I placed the invoice in my Bible, and Aunzo and I

prayed together every day that the Lord would supply the needed funds. The last day of the month came and went, but no money had become available. I was upset. The rule in the Mission was that all bills must be paid by the end of each month. It was, of course, a huge bill in my eyes, but we had reminded the Lord that it really was nothing to Him, perhaps the price of one cow, and are not 'the cattle on a thousand hills' His (Ps. 50:10)?

That Saturday morning, the first day of the new month, when I had received no mail, no money, no sign of any deliverance, there may have been a touch of bitterness in my thoughts. Had God let me down? I did not know what to do.

As I was returning home from the clinic at lunchtime, Aunzo met me excitedly. Waving a brown manila envelope at me, he blurted out: 'Mr Cripps [another missionary at Ibambi, who worked in the print-shop] sent this across for you. He said it came to him in his post yesterday, and he only noticed today that it had your name on it. Perhaps,' Aunzo hardly dared to add his suggestion, 'perhaps it is the money for the medicines for our clinic!'

We opened the envelope together and drew out the enclosed money and the statement of account from my Field-Leader. Aunzo piled and counted the money; I looked at the account. The total came to 4,800 Belgian Congo francs. The tithe of that would be 480 francs, leaving 4,320 francs – the exact sum we needed. I could hardly believe it. I looked at the names of the donors and realised that two of the three gifts had taken three or four months to reach me. Then I saw that they were labelled, 'This is for your leprosy work' – and yet, when they mailed their gifts and designated them I had not even intended opening a leprosy clinic! The ways of God are very wonderful and beyond the comprehension of men.

I wrote and thanked those donors, one couple of whom were quite unknown to me personally, one couple having met me once at a meeting before I came out to Zaire, and only one donor being well known to me. I felt awed to be the recipient of such prayerfully given gifts, where the donors were in such close touch with God that He could tell them exactly of the needs before I myself knew them. Truly they were spokes in God's wheel, channelling God's gifts to me as their part of the rim and they certainly entered deeply into fellowship with me in the work that God had given me to do.

In 1964, shortly before the outbreak of the civil war in the Congo, there was an amazing occasion when a large truck drove into our hospital compound and delivered over four tons of medical supplies. We presumed that it had been sent either by the World Health Organization or by the Catholic Aid Programme, CARITAS. It arrived at a critical moment of need. There was no note with it. The medicines had obviously been gathered from every conceivable source, many labels being printed not only in foreign languages, but also in strange scripts practically unintelligible to us. We sorted, re-labelled in Swahili and stacked on to shelves all the welcome supplies, though a little disappointed that the most needed drugs – antibiotics, analgesics and antimalarials – were only conspicuous because of their absence.

Seeking to decipher the contents of two cartons, each of 24 pint-sized intra-venous drip bottles, after much difficulty I was eventually fairly convinced that the solution was for treating a rare type of food-poisoning with severe respiratory distress. We sadly labelled the two boxes as such and relegated them to the back of the top shelf, such food-poisoning being virtually unknown to our tribal people.

That very week, some eight kilometres from our hospital, the villagers, running short of food during a wedding feast, had gathered, cooked and distributed wild yams to the guests. Within six hours, the whole village was gravely ill with food-poisoning, one symptom being severe respiratory distress. Over twenty people died before we could help them. Of those who managed to reach us, forty-eight of the most severely ill were treated with the intra-venous drip solution, gratefully retrieved from the back of the top shelf in the pharmacy: and they lived.

God's ways are truly mysterious and awesome. I have no doubt that most of those forty-eight would have died without that particular medical aid which I had never owned before, and never received again. It had arrived the very week that the need arose, and to this day we do not know who sent it, and have never been able to thank the donors – spokes in God's wheel, bringing the supply from our Hub, God Himself, to our bit of the rim at Nebobongo Hospital.

Then there was the occasion when I had to operate on Rebeka to help in the birth of her fifth child. She was the Christian wife of a MuBari evangelist, and her four previous children had all died at birth. At the same time, a teenage MuBari girl from the same village as Rebeka was having surgery in a non-mission hospital to the north of us. Sadly this girl died of a disastrous haemorrhage during surgery, whilst Rebeka, for whom much prayer had been made, survived and was delivered of a lovely healthy baby boy. First the body of the teenage girl, accompanied by her weeping mother, was returned to that pagan village some ninety kilometres to the south of our hospital; then twelve weeks later, Rebeka and her husband, with their new-born baby, walked home to the same village. As a result, the whole village of over eighty adults gave their hearts to the Saviour.

It was incredible! They had heard the Gospel for years but had been completely unresponsive. What had turned their hearts, suddenly to accept the truth? God had stepped into the situation in a way that they understood perfectly, even though we, with our western arrogance, could not at first comprehend. Their thought pattern is based on a logic of parallelism, and they saw not only that the pagan girl, going to a pagan hospital, undergoing surgery, had died, but also that

the Christian lady, going to a Christian hospital, also
undergoing surgery, had lived. Therefore the 'gods' of
the latter patient were stronger and more worthy of
worship than those of the former.

Obviously, I had been involved in this story, as I had
performed the operation for Rebeka: but when I oper-
ated on her, it was with no thought of being responsible
for a whole village turning to Christ! At the time they
were tremendously grateful to me but, within the space
of a few years, I am sure the tribe had forgotten the part I
played in bringing God's light into their darkness. They
grew in the Christian faith and became responsible in
their turn for reaching out to surrounding villages and
preaching the Gospel to others. I had been a 'spoke'
at the right moment, in the right place, linking our
Almighty Hub to that particular section of the rim.
God's purpose had been fulfilled. The spoke could now
disappear from view. It did not need to be endlessly
thanked; it could happily be forgotten.

Are we willing so to enter into God's purpose for the
part of the world where we are situated, that whether
thanked or not, whether noticed or ignored, we can just
be channels, available to Him for His strength and love
and compassion to pour through us to those in need?
Are we then equally willing to disappear from view and
be moved on to the next area of need?

Does God have to explain to us what He is doing or
why He wants us in any particular spot at any particular
time, or are we so given over to Him that He can use
us or not as He chooses? Can He rely on and trust us to
be a spoke and then ignore us while He deals with the
rim? Is it sufficient thanks just to know that we have
been there and been of use?

Furthermore, are we living in such close relationship
with the Hub that we can feel His heartbeat and sense
His pain at the suffering of our world? Are we willing to
be drawn up into that pain, even without explanation:
willing to watch with Him and ache with Him, without
falling asleep in our Garden of Gethsemane? The world

needs those who can empathise with its suffering, who can sit where they sit and hurt where they hurt, and then minister to them of the comfort of God. Can He lean on us and know we won't let Him down or fail them?

6

The Cup: the Practice of the Fellowship of Christ's Sufferings

> I want to know Christ and the power of his resur-
> rection and the fellowship of sharing in his suffer-
> ings, becoming like him in his death. (Phil. 3:10)

'Within the Veil': be this, beloved, thy portion,
Within the secret of thy Lord to dwell;
Beholding Him, until thy face His glory,
Thy life His love, thy lips His praise shall tell.

'Within the Veil,' for only as thou gazest
Upon the matchless beauty of His face,
Canst thou become a living revelation
Of His great heart of love, His untold grace.

'Within the Veil,' His fragrance poured upon thee,
Without the Veil, that fragrance shed abroad;
'Within the Veil,' His hand shall tune the music
Which sounds on earth the praises of thy Lord.

'Within the Veil,' thy spirit deeply anchored,
Thou walkest calm above a world of strife;
'Within the Veil' thy soul with Him united,
Shall live on earth His resurrection life.

Freda Hanbury Allen

At the beginning of the last chapter we asked the question: Are we willing to enter into the 'fellowship of God's sufferings'?

Leaving the picture language of the bicycle wheel, let us, in this final chapter, look more closely at this amazing thought that Almighty God condescends to invite us, His children, to share in the fellowship of His sufferings. This will form the third side of the triangle that we have been creating to represent the practical outworking of our relationships – and so of our fellowship – with God and with our fellow-men. This third side will unite all aspects of these into an indestructible whole.

When we thought of the first side of this triangle of fellowship, it signified to us the essential relationship of each one of us to God Himself. We took the yoke as our symbol of that union and of its outworking in the practicalities of daily life. The yoke spoke to us of submissive obedience, and consequently of the need for the sacrifice (if we can call it such) of our self-sufficiency.

We then thought of the second side of the triangle as signifying our relationship to – and so our fellowship with – other people, and we took the towel as our symbol. The towel spoke to us of servant-humility, and so of the need for the sacrifice of our self-pride as we seek to live out this relationship.

The final, third side of our triangle is going to speak to us of God's relationship with all people in His world, and His desire to draw us up into fellowship with Him in His suffering for that world. We shall take as our third symbol the cup. We shall see the cup as the symbol of suffering as well as of fellowship, and in it we shall see the need for the sacrifice of our independence and of our preferred freedom from such suffering.

The yoke revealed the paradox that in submission *to* Christ, we find our greatest freedom; the towel, that in service *for* Christ, we exercise the greatest authority. Now we shall see that the cup also offers us a paradox, that in suffering *with* Christ, we are perfected for glory.

In seeking to understand the real meaning of biblical *koinonia*, most often translated as fellowship, we have thought firstly of the basic, essential need for each individual to be directly related to God as children to their Father. Let us underline again that this is only achieved through the sacrifice of our Lord and Saviour on the Cross of Calvary.

Secondly, we have seen that He asks us to have fellowship with, and therefore to relate to, our fellow-men in an attitude of service. In fact, this second side of our triangle can be seen as God Himself relating to others *through* us.

Now we come, thirdly, to this yet-deeper level of truth, not now that of God relating to others *through* us, but of God relating directly to others, and inviting us to be drawn up into that relationship (indicated by the third side of our triangle) as we seek to enter into and share in His sufferings for them. Thus God offers us the inestimable privilege of sharing in the fellowship of His sufferings.

The cup is, without doubt, often thought of as a symbol of fellowship. When visitors arrive at our door, we invite them in and offer them a cup of tea. That is our way of saying that they are welcome and we wish to enjoy fellowship with them. When Jesus ate the Passover Feast with His disciples in the Upper Room, He passed the cup round and invited each one to drink of it with Him, as a symbol of fellowship. 'In the same way, after supper he took the cup, saying, "This cup is the new covenant in my blood; do this, whenever you drink it, in remembrance of me"' (1 Cor. 11:25).

But the cup is also a symbol of suffering. A few days before that meal together in the Upper Room, as they were journeying together towards Jerusalem, James and John came to Jesus:

> 'Teacher,' they said, 'we want you to do for us whatever we ask.'
>
> 'What do you want me to do for you?' he asked.
>
> They replied, 'Let one of us sit at your right and the other at your left in your glory.'
>
> 'You don't know what you are asking,' Jesus said. 'Can you drink the cup I drink or be baptised with the baptism I am baptised with?'
>
> 'We can,' they answered.
>
> Jesus said to them, 'You will drink the cup I drink and be baptised with the baptism I am baptised with, but to sit at my right or left is not for me to grant. These places belong to those for whom they have been prepared' (Mark 10:35–40).

'Can you drink of this cup?' Jesus asked them, and without doubt He was referring to His sufferings – intense sufferings – that were to fall upon Him within a few hours.

After having shared the cup of fellowship with them around the table at the Passover Feast, Jesus was praying in agony in the Garden of Gethsemane. He cried to His Father, 'My Father, if it is possible, may this cup be taken from Me . . . ' (Matt. 26:39). Clearly, here, this was the cup of suffering, suffering such as we can barely conceive of, with its weight and horror and gross darkness. Yet He took that cup and drank it to the dregs for us and for all mankind.

There cannot be two different interpretations of the cup of which Christ spoke three times within the space of twenty-four hours. It must be the same cup, and so we have to accept that the Cup of Fellowship that He offers us, as a memorial of His shed blood, is also the Cup of Suffering from which He shrank in the Garden.

We are not considering those things which *we* think of as sufferings. We are not asking God to fellowship with us in our sufferings – the sufferings, physical and mental, of sickness and sadness that are common to all mankind; nor of the suffering caused by guilt and by the consequent loneliness and fear that are common to all sinners; nor even of suffering such as distress for our own failures and unworthiness, burdens for unsaved relatives and friends; nor indeed the grievous sense of inadequacy before the pain of the world that is common to all Christians.

No! We are now speaking of *His* sufferings, and the fact that He actually condescends to seek our fellowship, that we would stand with Him and support Him in all that grieves and pains His heart. In the Garden of Gethsemane, Jesus took His three closest friends a stone's throw further on than the rest, that they might be near to Him in His hour of greatest need. He sought their support, believing that they would watch with Him and pray for Him, endeavouring to enter into His agony and bear Him up.

And they slept. 'Then he returned to his disciples and found them sleeping. "Could you men not keep watch with me for one hour?" he asked Peter' (Matt. 26:40).

What were, what are, His sufferings, in which He invites us to share in deep, intimate fellowship? His sufferings are so different from our often self-inflicted problems.

He suffers deep pain from the sin of mankind. As

He lived and walked here on this earth, He must have suffered deeply from what He saw and heard of the filth, the obscenities and the cruelties that are enacted by people against each other – not just the obvious sin, but also the sin we allow in our thought-life and in our imaginations; the sin of jealousy and envy that promote wickedness and cruelty; the sin of self-indulgence and the desire to exercise power over others that corrupts so much of our society; the sin of greed, and ambition that stops at nothing to achieve its own ends, no matter who suffers in the process. In the presence of sin, our Saviour suffers.

As He anticipated the Cross, He suffered the agony of knowing that in becoming our sin, He would have to be separated from fellowship with His Father. From eternity to eternity, Christ the Son and God the Father are One. All through His earthly life, the Son spent hours alone in communion with His Father, out on the mountains, often throughout a whole night, just tasting the sweetness of being One. The thought of that dread moment of separation, when He would cry out in anguish, 'My God, my God, why have you forsaken me?' (Matt. 27:46), must have caused our Lord a depth of suffering of which we know nothing.

He accepted His Father's will for His self to go to death on the Cross and to descend into hell to carry away our sin. And yet, throughout those last few days, even His closest friends totally misunderstood Him, arguing among themselves as to who would be the greatest in heaven. They all fled from Him, leaving Him unutterably alone to face His enemies and persecutors. Men scorned Him or were indifferent to Him, despised Him and spat upon Him, even as He moved forward to complete their salvation, crying out on their behalf, 'Father, forgive them, for they do not know what they are doing' (Luke 23:34).

What do we know of fellowship with Christ in *these* sufferings?

'Look, the Lamb of God, who takes away the sin of the world!' (John 1:29).

As we gaze at the Lamb – the loneliest Man who ever walked this earth, as He went alone to Calvary, deserted by all whom He loved; a Man abused by all mankind, smitten, flogged, mocked, spat upon, despised and rejected; misunderstood and falsely accused beyond all conceivable measure, without ever retaliating or seeking to defend Himself; betrayed by the kiss of a friend and butchered to death by cruel soldiers and an indifferent crowd – our complacency must be shaken, to think that He, the Lamb, suffered so deeply for us, and actually yearns for our companionship in that suffering.

Am I too involved elsewhere to watch with Him? Am I too busy serving Him and fulfilling the programme I have set myself to have time just to be with Him? Am I too preoccupied with my own holiness to be able to share with Him as He wants me to?

Am I too scared as to what might happen to my self, so that I am not free to follow Him all the way to Calvary – as Peter was, warming himself by the soldiers' fire, and frightened by a young servant girl until he swore and cursed, saying he had never known Jesus? Am I afraid that I might become too deeply involved in His suffering to be able to extricate myself, if I followed Him more closely and openly?

Jesus had nowhere to lay His head, He had no way of escape, He had no one to understand and sympathise with Him. He was alone.

> 'I looked, but there was no-one to help,
> I was appalled that no-one gave support.'
>
> (Isa. 63.5)

'I looked for a man among them who would build up the wall and stand before me in the gap . . . but I found none' (Ezek. 22:30).

Oh, so alone! Where was I? Where am I today? Will I too leave Him all alone to carry the weight of sorrow for the sin of this world; or will I dare to respond to His invitation to join in His sorrow and share fellowship with Him in the way that He shall choose?

Again, in this chapter we are going to ask ourselves the same three questions that we asked when we thought of the yoke and of the towel.

> With whom are we invited to suffer?
> Why must we suffer with Him?
> How do we share in His sufferings?

With whom are we invited to suffer?

Amazing thought! The great Almighty Creator God Himself – who gave His only begotten Son to suffer death on the Cross for our redemption – invites us to share with *Him*.

The meaning of the Cross was revealed to the children of Israel in the early chapters of the Scriptures, when Abraham was called by God to sacrifice his son, his beloved son Isaac. Abraham was doubtless startled. Could this really be the voice of God, or was it some enemy trying to deceive him? Had not God given Isaac to Sarah and himself in their old age, a child who was to inherit all God's promises given to them, a child in whose progeny all the nations of the world were to be blessed?

If . . . did the doubts and fears begin to circle through Abraham's puzzled mind? If he sacrificed Isaac, who would inherit the promises? God had said that in him the blessing would be passed on to succeeding generations – how could this be, if he died now? But if he did not obey God's voice, how could he continue in His favour? Life held nothing for him if he embarked on disobedience. Some thirty years before, he had disobeyed God in an endeavour to bring about His purposes, and this self-determined act had cost him thirteen years of silence, thirteen years of lost fellowship, and he never wanted that to occur again.

So on that dread day, some 4,000 years ago, Abraham stepped out in blind obedience to God, trusting that He would somehow bring about a satisfactory outcome. He took his son Isaac, firewood and fire, cords and a knife. Together with his servants, the little convoy started out on mules towards the mountains. Nearing their destination, Abraham left the servants and the mules, and he and his son went forward together on foot. The teenage youth was puzzled and asked his father a question:

'Father . . . the fire and wood are here,' Isaac said, 'but where is the lamb for the burnt offering?'

Abraham answered, 'God Himself will provide the lamb for the burnt offering, my son' (Gen. 22:7–8).

Having arrived at the place to which God had directed him, Abraham and Isaac built the altar and laid the wood in order. Abraham then bound his son and laid him on the wood, and prepared to sacrifice him as he believed God had commanded him to do – willing, in obedience, to give his dearest and best, if that should be the will of the Eternal.

The voice of the Angel of the Lord rang out and arrested him, knife upraised, and prevented him completing the act – and there behind him was a ram, caught in the thicket, and Abraham sacrificed the ram in the place of his son Isaac. As it is recorded in Hebrews:

By faith Abraham, when God tested him, offered Isaac as a sacrifice . . . his one and only son, even though God had said to him, 'It is through Isaac that your offspring will be reckoned.' Abraham reasoned that God could raise the dead, and figuratively speaking, he did receive Isaac back from death (Heb. 11:17–19).

So was enacted the closest human analogy possible to the predetermined plan of God, who 'so loved the world that he gave his one and only Son,' to die on Calvary, 'that whoever believes in him shall not perish but have eternal life' (John 3:16); Jesus 'was raised on the third day according to the Scriptures' (1 Cor. 15:4).

Why did God Almighty suffer for us in such a way? How did we come to cause Him such suffering?

If we go back to the beginning of the story of man, we see that God, who created man, wanted to have fellowship with him. God walked in the Garden in the cool of the day, to converse with Adam and Eve and to enjoy being with them. But, having eaten the fruit of the forbidden tree, they were ashamed and 'they hid from the Lord God among the trees of the garden' (Gen. 3:8).

And so, through all the succeeding generations, we men and women of every tribe on earth, through the shame and guilt of sin, have hidden ourselves from God. We have erected barriers – barriers not only of bamboo and iron, but also of human wisdom and wealth – in an attempt to shut God out, to pretend He isn't there, rather than face up to our guilt, loneliness and insecurity. We put on an outward appearance of great ability and cocksure self-sufficiency, rather than acknowledge our need of the Supreme Creator and our longing for fellowship with Him. We were created to be in close communion with Him and we are incomplete without that fellowship; and no amount of logical reasoning and scientific argument can ultimately satisfy our heart's hunger.

God wants our fellowship – and we hide from Him in shame.

God wants our obedience, as a mark of our love. No amount of protestations of love can be an expression of the truth while we are living in disobedience. God gave Adam and Eve one little command, as a means for them to show their love – by their willingness to forgo their liberty to choose their own way, and to accept His right to their obedience – thereby demonstrating love in its purest form. But their natural curiosity and desire for personal liberty was so strong that they rejected God's right to their lives and to their love; and so they destroyed themselves, and turned godly love into self-love, which has poisoned us all ever since.

After their repeated request to be like all other nations, God gave the children of Israel a king. He then sought to prove King Saul, as to whether he would lead the nation according to His laws. The prophet Samuel was commanded to send Saul on an errand to enact God's judgment on the Amalekites following their refusal to help the children of Israel. Saul fulfilled nine-tenths of God's command but, in the last analysis, he failed to complete the obedience, keeping the best sheep and oxen alive and also sparing the life of the king himself. When Samuel met him returning from the battle, Saul declared:

'I have carried out the Lord's instructions.'

But Samuel said: 'What then is this bleating of sheep in my ears? What is this lowing of cattle that I hear?'

Saul answered, 'The soldiers brought them from the Amalekites; they spared the best of the sheep and cattle to sacrifice to the Lord your God, but we totally destroyed the rest . . . '

But Samuel replied:

> Does the Lord delight in burnt
> offerings and sacrifices
> as much as in obeying the
> voice of the Lord?
> To obey is better than sacrifice,
> and to heed is better than
> the fat of rams.

(1 Sam. 15:13–22)

Have we not behaved in a similar way, all down the ages? We have wanted to show God our love by a way that we choose and that pleases us. We have thought our so-called sacrifices would please Him. We have considered that the size of our annual offering would impress Him. We cannot believe that our enthusiasm and zeal in singing of our love for God might not be acceptable to Him – who judges hearts rather than lips. We also have sought to shift the blame on to others – 'the soldiers spared them' Saul had said – when God has rejected our platitudes.

God wants our obedience – and we want to gratify our own desires.

God wants, above all else, that we should worship Him. He prepared ways for that worship that were pleasing and acceptable to Himself. He gave Moses a wonderful and detailed vision of the Tabernacle, 'the tent of Meeting', and Moses had it made and erected 'according to the pattern shown [him] on the mountain' (Ex. 25:40). God then gave Moses a detailed explanation as to how men were to approach Him in that Tabernacle in order to worship Him in a worthy manner. No one was to approach Him without the offering of a blood sacrifice, and the animal offered was to be without blemish. With amazing detail, reflecting all the varying aspects and meaning of the Sacrifice of His Son on Calvary, the different offerings were instituted.

Besides all of which, there were regulations for transporting the Tabernacle from place to place when the campsite was moved. There were detailed laws given as to how it was to be dismantled, carried and re-erected in the next campsite. All this ceremonial was to ensure that the worship of the people would be acceptable to God.

But time passed. The people felt that the laws were a little cumbersome, and possibly somewhat irrelevant now that they were a settled people and no longer nomadic. The endless sacrificing of animals was not only expensive but also a bit crude and smelly – had they not matured and grown up now, so that they could use a somewhat simpler form of worship, less costly and time-consuming, but equally pleasing?

In an earlier chapter, we thought of the story of the bringing back of the Ark of the Covenant, which had been captured in battle by the Philistines, in order to restore it to its proper resting place in the Temple in Jerusalem. At their first attempt they failed, because they sought to worship God according to that which was pleasing to themselves; at their second attempt, when they sought to obey God in every minutest detail, they succeeded. As they fulfilled the law of God, and worshipped Him in the manner that He Himself had ordained, their worship was acceptable to the Almighty and He blessed them.

God wants our worship, but so often we want to give it in our own chosen way, without reference to God's prescribed way, pleasing to us but not necessarily worthy of Him.

God wants our love – in fellowship, obedience and worship – and is willing to pour His love into our hearts so that we can love Him in a manner of which He is worthy. But with independent hearts we so often want to express things in our own way.

As Jesus approached Jerusalem, shortly before the Feast of the Passover, He was surrounded by a tremendous crowd who were all going up for the great ceremony; and they worshipped Him.

> Many people spread their cloaks on the road, while others spread branches they had cut in the fields. Those who went ahead and those who followed shouted,
>
> > 'Hosanna!'
> >
> > 'Blessed is he who comes in the name of the Lord!'
> >
> > 'Blessed is the coming kingdom of our father David!'
> >
> > 'Hosanna in the highest!'
> > > (Mark 11:8–10)

Yet less than a week later, when Pilate asked the same crowd if he should not release Jesus, they turned against Him:

> With one voice they cried out, 'Away with this man! Release Barabbas to us!' (Barabbas had been thrown into prison for an insurrection in the city, and for murder.)
> Wanting to release Jesus, Pilate appealed to them again. But they kept shouting, 'Crucify him! Crucify him!' (Luke 23:18–21).

Over the centuries, whenever our worship of God has deteriorated into an emotional or sentimental self-pleasing ritual, our desire for holiness and our hunger to know God intimately have also waned. Once again we too, at least metaphorically, may be found crying with the rabble: 'Crucify him, crucify him!'

Yes, God wants our love, but can it be that instead we offer Him our hatred?

God loved us so deeply, purely and immeasurably, and with a love that passes all understanding in its breadth, length, depth and height, that He actually *planned* His own suffering. Before He had even created us men and women, we read that God had planned Calvary, 'before the foundation of the world'. Can one suggest, reverently, that perhaps God had a vision of people to love, worship and obey Him, to be to the praise of His glory, to walk with Him and talk with Him – people with whom He, Almighty God, could enjoy fellowship? 'They will need a place to live,' God must have mused – and so He created the world and all that was needed for us to live. 'They will need free will, so that they can choose to love Me,' God may have further reasoned within the Trinity – and so He created humankind in His own image with the ability to choose – to choose to obey or disobey, and so to love God or to love self. And God knew that some would choose to love self. He would have known from the beginning that for

His plan to succeed laws would be needed, and one of the fundamental ones would have to be: 'The wages of sin is death.' So God foresaw that His special creation – people to love Him and with whom He could enjoy fellowship – would choose death.

How could this be prevented, and yet at the same time leave men free to make the necessary choice? If man did not have free will, how could he love? Love is only love when it is free to choose to love. Love that is obligatory is not love. A robot cannot love. So man must keep his free will. But how to prevent him from misusing it? Or when he has misused it, and chosen the path that leads to spiritual death – eternal separation from the holy Lord God – how can his sin be forgiven and put away without decreasing God's holiness and righteousness? If God merely forgave 'because He loved,' that would make nonsense of His laws.

So God planned Calvary. There was no other way. Someone had to die, because people by their disobedience earned death. The only possible Substitute, who could accept the wages in place of humankind, would have to be sinless, and able to die. But there is no one without sin, except God Himself: 'For all have sinned and fall short of the glory of God' (Rom. 3:23). 'There is no-one righteous, not even one' (Rom. 3:10). But how could God die in our place? God cannot die – He is Spirit. Then God conceived the amazing and audacious plan that He, God, would become Man in order to die in our place, as our substitute, as the perfect ransom:

> There was no other good enough
> To pay the price of sin:
> He only could unlock the gates
> Of heaven and let us in.
>
> Cecil Francis Alexander (1823–95)

So God planned that the Word should become flesh and dwell among men in order to be obedient, obedient unto death, obedient unto death upon a Cross.

Then – and only then – having thought out the whole magnificent plan of our redemption, did God actually create Man.

Only Almighty God could have conceived such a wonderful plan – so utterly simple and yet so profoundly comprehensive, so totally sufficient and capable of satisfying all the demands of holiness and mercy. Only Almighty God would have conceived such a plan where He, God, pays the whole price and we, the sinners, receive the whole benefit. To us, redemption was to be a free gift; to God, it cost Him His dearest and His best, His only begotten Son.

> Oh, the love that drew Salvation's plan:
> Oh, the grace that brought it down to man:
> Oh, the mighty gulf that God did span
> – at Calvary.

William R. Newell (*CSSM Choruses*)

So we see that God planned His own suffering on our behalf because He so loved us. To ask, 'Why does a God of love allow suffering?' is nonsensical when we realise that because He is a God of love, He suffers. Had He not loved us, He would not have suffered for us. His love caused Him to suffer. The two are inextricably one. True godly love will always involve suffering. If we don't want to suffer, we must not seek to love. Love will lead us into suffering, just because that is its nature.

God loved us so much that He wanted to have fellowship with us – to walk with us and talk with us. He planned that we should worship, love and obey Him as a manifestation of that fellowship. But we changed God's plan by misusing our free will; and to restore the relationship, so that He could again enjoy the fellowship, God embarked on a road of unbelievable suffering. The depths of God's love can be measured by the depths of His suffering.

Again we must ask ourselves, 'With whom are we
invited to suffer?' Not only is it the Almighty Lord
God who dares to invite us to share in His sufferings,
but also it is the Holy Son of God. 'Christ suffered for
you, leaving you an example . . . ' (1 Pet. 2:21).

Let us try to understand in what ways He suffered.
Indeed, *why* did He suffer?

The Son of God suffered as He looked down from
the glory of Heaven and viewed the state of the world
– the world that He and His Father had created to be
the dwelling place of man, where man could worship
Him in perfect fellowship.

The Son of God suffered the humiliation of being
born, as one would say, 'out of wedlock', to the Virgin
Mary. Even the vast majority of her friends would think
of her as an adulteress, and of Him as a bastard.

He suffered the poverty of the stable, with the smell
of cattle-dung and damp straw, rather than the sweet
fragrance of the beauty of His heavenly home. He
suffered the daily routine chores of the carpenter's shop,
living among the poor and disadvantaged in Nazareth.

His pure soul would have suffered every time He
heard swear words and coarse jokes, every time He
saw brutality to man or beast, every time He met with
cheating and swindling, sickness and sorrow, in the
narrow streets of His environment as He grew up into
manhood.

His heart will have suffered as He saw the miser-
able lot of women, the wickedness of the nation, the
drunkenness and debauchery of soldiers, the treachery
of authorities and the insurrection of the rabble.

His innermost being must have suffered when His
own beloved disciples misunderstood Him, arguing
among themselves, seeking out personal promotion
and filled with selfish ambitions.

He wept over Jerusalem:

'O Jerusalem, Jerusalem, you who kill the prophets
and stone those sent to you, how often I have

longed to gather your children together, as a hen
gathers her chicks under her wings, but you were
not willing!' (Matt. 23:37)

He groaned in spirit and was troubled at the graveside
of Lazarus, simply because they could not, would not,
understand His message. He was deeply distressed
when He came down from the Mount of Transfiguration and met the powerlessness of His disciples to
heal the epileptic boy, and realised that they had not
understood what He had been teaching them. He was
grieved when Peter, having just declared that He was
the Christ, the Son of the living God, then tried to
protect Him by preventing Him from going up to
Jerusalem to be crucified. Peter and the others had
not understood His mission.

After a long journey on foot from Jerusalem towards
Galilee, He suffered thirst and weariness in order to reach
out to one woman, a Samaritan woman, a woman despised
and cast out by her own people but loved by God.

He was so poor that, when teaching one day, He had
to borrow a penny for an illustration; He had to borrow
a donkey to ride into Jerusalem; He had nowhere to
lay His head, and even after death, He had to borrow
another's grave.

He suffered insults and derision, strikings and false
testimony, betrayal by Judas, denial by Peter, desertion
by all His closest friends, forsaken and alone in the hour
of His greatest need of fellowship and help.

Physically, mentally, spiritually, Jesus must have
suffered more than any other person has ever suffered.
He was 'tempted in every way just as we are' – in every
part of His being, relentlessly and cunningly, Satan
using every device and trick of his trade to trap the
Holy One and bring Him down in the eyes of men
– 'yet [He] was without sin' (Heb. 4:15). He never
gave in, He never accepted a moment's respite from
temptation by yielding to it; He fought hell's legions
undismayed to the bitter end.

When we pray to share in the fellowship of His sufferings, this is something of what we are speaking: but oh, there is so much more!

As we saw briefly in Chapter Four, Isaiah tells us something of the deeper suffering of the Messiah:

He grew up before him [God] like a tender shoot,
   and like a root out of dry ground.
He had no beauty or majesty to attract us to him,
   nothing in his appearance that we should
      desire him.
He was despised and rejected by men,
   a man of sorrows, and familiar with suffering.
Like one from whom men hide their faces
   he was despised, and we esteemed him not.

Surely he took up our infirmities
   and carried our sorrows,
yet we considered him stricken by God,
   smitten by him, and afflicted.
But he was pierced for our transgressions,
   he was crushed for our iniquities;
the punishment that brought us peace
      was upon him,
   and by his wounds we are healed.
We all, like sheep, have gone astray,
   each of us has turned to his own way;
and the Lord has laid on him
   the iniquity of us all.

He was oppressed and afflicted,
   yet he did not open his mouth;
he was led like a lamb to the slaughter,
   and as a sheep before her shearers
      is silent,
   so he did not open his mouth.
By oppression and judgment he was taken
      away.
   And who can speak of his descendants?

For he was cut off from the land of the
    living;
  for the transgression of my people he
    was stricken.
He was assigned a grave with the wicked,
  and with the rich in his death,
though he had done no violence,
  nor was any deceit in his mouth.

(Isa. 53:2–9)

In John's Gospel, chapter 12, Jesus likens Himself to a
grain of wheat:

'The hour has come for the Son of Man to be
glorified. I tell you the truth, unless a grain of
wheat falls to the ground and dies, it remains only
a single seed. But if it dies, it produces many seeds.
The man who loves his life will lose it, while the
man who hates his life in this world will keep it
for eternal life. Whoever serves me must follow
me; and where I am, my servant also will be. My
Father will honour the one who serves me.
  Now my heart is troubled, and what shall I say?
"Father, save me from this hour"? No, it was for
this very reason I came to this hour. Father, glorify
your name' (John 12:23–8).

'My hour is come!' Jesus cried out, knowing He was
on the last stretch of the road mapped out for Him by
His Father to bring about our salvation. The ultimate
horror for Him was only a few hours away. On the
Cross, His Father would indeed be glorified – by Jesus'
obedience, and by His perfect revelation of His Father's
character – His abhorrence and hatred of sin and yet
His intense love for the sinner.
  Christ saw Himself as the corn of wheat which had
to fall into the ground and die, if it were ever to bring
forth a harvest. As He died, was buried and rose again,

He would be able to bring many sons to glory. Calvary would result in the harvest of Pentecost, when 3,000 souls would be added to the Church.

Then He came to the crux of His heartbroken outburst: 'My heart is troubled!' and we can catch a glimpse into His innermost being. Dare we try to understand even a tiny fraction of what He suffered for us in the next twenty-four hours of His life? As we humbly look on, surely it must increase our love for Him and our willingness to be identified with Him, even to die to ourselves that others might live.

In the Gospel records of the scene in the Garden of Gethsemane, at the trial and at the place of crucifixion, there are seven Greek words used to speak of the agony of distress in Christ's heart. Let us briefly savour those words, even if we can only do so to a very limited extent, that we might seek to enter in and understand His sufferings there.

Firstly, Luke tells us that He was 'straitened', 'I have a baptism to undergo, and how distressed [straitened (AV)] I am until it is completed!' (Luke 12:50), and we have a picture of someone in a straitjacket, pinioned, unable to move or to make a decision, bound round on all sides by the desperateness of the situation. We could picture a bird held in a tiny cage, with no room to flap his wings, frustrated and frightened, his environment wholly foreign to him.

Then John records for us the Saviour's words, 'Now my heart is troubled' (John 12:27). His heart was in utter consternation, knowing what was His Father's will and yet deeply fearful of the appalling physical, mental, human and spiritual cost that was to be involved. His Father's will – the price He had to pay – what if He were overcome by the latter so that He was unable to fulfil the former?

In Mark's record, we read that He was deeply distressed, troubled and overwhelmed with sorrow to the point of death. He [Jesus] took Peter, James and John along with Him, and He began to be deeply distressed and troubled. 'My soul is overwhelmed with sorrow to the point of death,' He said to them. 'Stay here and keep watch' (Mark 14:33–4). Jesus, the Man, in His humanity, became alarmed at the prospect of bearing the weight of the world's sin. He was sore amazed at the dawning realisation of the awfulness of the coming burden: one could almost say He was scared stiff.

The great heaviness that the disciples sensed in Him was akin to an overwhelming depression, a dejection that weighed Him down so alarmingly that He was near to fainting, unable to support it. 'My soul is overwhelmed with sorrow to the point of death.' He cried to them, crushed in spirit at what He saw lay ahead. So heavy was the burden that He feared He might die there in the Garden and never reach the Cross, and so fail to achieve His Father's purpose, our salvation. It was not the nails on the Cross that caused His death, but the shattering burden of our sin which necessitated the agony of His separation from His Father.

We turn to Luke's account of that tragic scene, and we tread very softly as we overhear the prayer of our Lord at the moment of His most poignant agony:

He withdrew about a stone's throw beyond them, knelt down and prayed, 'Father, if you are willing, take this cup from me; yet not my will, but yours, be done.' An angel from heaven appeared to him and strengthened him. And being in anguish, he prayed more earnestly, and his sweat was like drops of blood falling to the ground (Luke 22:41–4).

He pled with His Father that, if it were possible, the cup of suffering, pain and hurt should be taken away from Him. His holy being shrank from the awfulness of all that was involved. And yet, He added, possibly in a gasp of determination, 'Not my will, but yours, be done.' An angel strengthened Him so that He would not die of heartbreak, fear or physical weakness. He knew

He must go through with the terrible plan, and drink the cup to its dregs, if we were to be saved. 'Being in an agony' – the exquisite anguish of striving to complete the race that was set before Him caused His sweat to fall like great drops of blood.

Hanging on the Cross, in the darkest hour of spiritual agony and aloneness, we hear His piteous cry, 'My God, My God, why have you forsaken me?' (Matt. 27:45) Did He feel let down? Deserted even by His Father? Suddenly overwhelmingly alone? Did He suddenly sense that in very truth He had become our sin and so His Father, who was of purer eyes than to behold iniquity, had to turn His gaze away from Him? Did He somehow know that God His Father was leaving Him down in the ground, as the corn of wheat, to die? We cannot conjecture, we dare not seek to question too closely. It is indeed sacred ground, and we must take off our shoes. 'God made him [Jesus] who had no sin to be sin for us, so that in him we might become the righteousness of God' (2 Cor. 5:21). Profound theology, beyond the ability of our human minds to conceive, and yet the simplest Gospel, within the grasp of the youngest child to accept – oh, what a wonderful Saviour!

This is the *suffering* of Christ for us, that He might redeem us:

> Wounded for me, wounded for me,
> There on the Cross He was wounded for me.

> Rev. W. G. Ovens (*CSSM Choruses*, 1921)

He calls us to follow Him if we would be His disciples – all the way to Calvary.

Do I still wish to share in the fellowship of *His* sufferings?

Why must we suffer?

We have already considered the fact that we were

created to be containers, containers of the Spirit of God and not of the spirit of self, and that as containers we must *submit* to that which we contain. We have also considered that to contain in itself is not the fulfilment of God's purpose: we contain only in order that others may receive the contents. As we have already noted, a glass of cold water only fulfils its purpose when a needy person slakes his thirst. In order to *serve* others, the contents within the container are always spent. When the container is human and not inanimate, the loss of the contents often entails a degree of *suffering*.

As Christ was spent, pouring out His life for us on the Cross, He underwent quite horrific suffering. As He hung on the Cross pouring out His life on our behalf, His whole body racked with the seering pain of flogging and the excruciating pain of crucifixion, He cried out, 'I am thirsty' (John 19:28).

One remembers the terrible prophetic picture painted by the Psalmist:

Roaring lions tearing their prey
  open their mouths wide against me.
I am poured out like water,
  and all my bones are out of joint.
My heart has turned to wax;
  it has melted away within me.
My strength is dried up like a potsherd,
  and my tongue sticks to the roof of my mouth;
  you lay me in the dust of death.
Dogs have surrounded me;
  a band of evil men has encircled me,
  they have pierced my hands and my feet.
I can count all my bones;
  people stare and gloat over me.
They divide my garments among them
  and cast lots for my clothing.

(Psalm 22:13–18)

Dimly one can discern that the suffering was caused by the contents within the container being spent in the service of others. How truly our Lord and Saviour 'poured out his life unto death' (Isa. 53:12) – the perfect sinless life contained in the human frame of Jesus of Nazareth, poured out for the salvation of sinners, as He accepted the death we deserved as the wages for our sin.

And all this solely because of His great love for us (Eph. 2:4). Had He not loved us, He would not have died for us:

> . . . the Son of God, who loved me and gave himself for me (Gal. 2:20).

> This is how we know what love is: Jesus Christ laid down his life for us (1 John 3:16).

> This is how God showed his love among us: he sent his one and only Son into the world that we might live through him. This is love: not that we loved God, but that he loved us and sent his Son as an atoning sacrifice for our sins (1 John 4:9–10).

We would seem to have come full circle. We were created to be containers, that the contents might be spent in the service of others, and all this because we were created to love. Because we were created to love, I dare to suggest, we were created to suffer.

> He told them [His disciples], 'This is what is written: The Christ will suffer and rise from the dead on the third day,' translated in the Authorised Version as 'It behoved Christ to suffer' (Luke 24:46).

> 'The Son of Man must suffer' (Mark 8:31; 9:12).

If we are to follow in Christ's footsteps, we too will have to suffer. Did He not say, 'If any one would come after me, he must deny himself and take up his cross daily and follow me' (Luke 9:23), and He was on His way to the most terrible suffering imaginable, the crucifixion at Calvary. Dare we follow Him?

Peter also writes, 'To this you were called, because Christ suffered for you, leaving you an example, that you should follow in his steps' (1 Pet. 2:21).

We were created to love and worship God, and there-fore given our free will to enable us to choose to so do. God wishes to pour into us His love – for we love Him 'because he first loved us' (1 John 4:19) – so that we have wherewith to love Him! But if we are to receive His love in order to love Him and those around us, we have to reckon with the fact that it was His love for us that drove Him to suffer. The very love He pours into us is a love that suffers. We have to be willing and prepared to suffer if we would embrace His love. True love always leads to suffering: there is no escape. Only where men do not love, can they hope not to suffer.

As we seek to enter in and share in His sufferings, so He pours not only His love but also His comfort into our hearts. Then we have the wherewithal to comfort others who suffer:

> Praise be to the God and Father of our Lord Jesus Christ, the Father of compassion and the God of all comfort, who comforts us in all our troubles, so that we can comfort those in any trouble with the comfort we ourselves have received from God. For just as the sufferings of Christ flow over into our lives, so also through Christ our comfort overflows (2 Cor. 1:3–5).

Secondly, we were created to be holy. The fulfilment of this will also inevitably lead to suffering. Just as God's love in us will lead us into a fellowship with Him in His sufferings, so also will God's holiness.

As we seek to grow in the grace and knowledge of our Lord, we shall develop an ever-deepening hunger and thirst after righteousness, that we might be pleasing to Him in all things. He has promised that those who so hunger and thirst will be filled (Matt. 5:6), but He also promises us that if we thus seek after holiness, we shall suffer, 'In fact, everyone who wants to live a godly life in Christ Jesus will be persecuted' (2 Tim. 3:12), but then He adds:

> 'Blessed are those who are persecuted because of righteousness,
>   for theirs is the kingdom of heaven.'

(Matt. 5:10)

We should not seek to run away from or to avoid suffering: it is part of our heavenly Father's plan for our lives, to conform us to the image of His Son. Somehow, our attitude to suffering has become warped. We tend to think of all suffering – physical, mental, spiritual – as a bad thing, to be avoided at all costs. And if it does dare to approach us, we think we have the right to claim deliverance from it by the hand of our omnipotent God.

Christians in the first century had a very different idea, and it would seem to have been a much healthier attitude and more in line with the heart of God. New converts were taught to expect suffering as the natural outcome of being saved! Samuel Zwemer wrote, 'Jesus Christ never hid His scars to win disciples.' In fact, His scars were the only thing that Jesus showed to His disciples after the Resurrection as His badge of authority and authenticity, 'He showed them his hands and side' (John 20:20), as much as to say: If you follow Me, you must expect similar scars.

When God sent Ananias to Paul at Damascus, He told him, 'Go! This man is my chosen instrument to carry my name before the Gentiles and their kings and before the people of Israel. I will show him how much he must suffer for my name' (Acts 9:15–16). Paul was only a few days old as a Christian, yet he was to be told immediately of all that he would be called upon to suffer in becoming Christ's ambassador. First-century Christians had to be prepared to suffer not only mockery but also vicious cruelty from the hands of pagan authorities, torture and savagery from the hands of despotic rulers:

'Blessed are you when people insult you, persecute you and falsely say all kinds of evil against you because of me. Rejoice and be glad, because great is your reward in heaven, for in the same way they persecuted the prophets who were before you' (Matt. 5:11–12).

Jesus never deceived His disciples. They knew they would suffer if they followed Him. Had he not told them to take up their cross daily, deny themselves and forsake all others if they wanted to follow Him as His disciples? In fact, Christ's last command to them as He left them and ascended back into glory was, 'You will receive power when the Holy Spirit comes on you; and you will be my witnesses in Jerusalem, and in all Judea and Samaria, and to the ends of the earth' (Acts 1:8). The word He used to express the idea of witnesses was the Greek word *martus* – the implication surely being that to be a witness in those days would almost certainly end in martyrdom. To be His witnesses meant to reveal Him – to live as He lived, to show forth His character, to be holy as He is holy. Holy in the midst of a desperately unholy environment. Was it not Christ's pure and holy character that had, humanly, led Him to the Cross? If we are to display that same characteristic, in the same worldly atmosphere in which He lived, can we not expect a similar outcome? 'No servant is greater than his master,' Jesus said to His disciples. 'If they persecuted me, they will persecute you also' (John 15:20). The more I long to be like Jesus, particularly with regard to His perfect holiness and sinlessness, the more certainly I must expect to suffer, 'For it has been granted to you on behalf of Christ not only to believe on him, but also to suffer for him, since you are going through the same struggle you saw I had, and now hear that I still have,' wrote Paul to the Philippian Christians, from his prison cell in Rome (Phil. 1:29–30).

Is the world crying out to us, His servants, 'Show us your hands!'? What have we to show? Do we 'always carry around in our body the death of Jesus, so that the life of Jesus may also be revealed in our body' as Paul wrote to the Corinthians (2 Cor. 4:10)? Or is it, as Amy Carmichael wrote, that we have no scars?

> Hast thou no scar?
> No hidden scar on foot, or side, or hand?
> I hear thee sung as mighty in the land,
> I hear them hail thy bright ascendant star.
> Hast thou no scar?
>
> Hast thou no wound?
> Yet I was wounded by the archers, spent,
> Leaned me against a tree to die; and rent
> By ravenous beasts that compassed Me, I swooned.
> Hast thou no wound?
>
> No wound? No scar?
> Yet, as the Master shall the servant be,
> And pierced are the feet that follow Me;
> But thine are whole; can he have followed far
> Who has nor wound nor scar?

I believe it is Christ's greatest desire that in knowing Him we should be like Him, and therefore willing to share in the fellowship of His sufferings. As Amy Carmichael wrote:

> 'Have I been so long time with thee
> And yet hast thou not known Me?'
>
> Blessed Master I have known Thee
> On the roads of Galilee.

'Have I been so long time with thee
On the roads of Galilee:
Yet, My child, has thou not known Me
When I walked upon the sea?'

Blessed Master, I have known Thee
On the roads and on the sea.

'Wherefore then hast thou not known Me
Broken in Gethsemane?

'I would have thee follow, know Me
Thorn-crowned, nailed upon the Tree.
Canst thou follow, wilt thou know Me
All the way to Calvary?'

Thirdly, we were created to be with Christ in glory. But to fulfil that purpose, we must suffer.

What is glory? Is it not the revelation of the excellent character of God? Is that not why, when Jesus died on Calvary, He supremely manifested God's glory?

Jesus replied, 'The hour has come for the Son of Man to be glorified' . . .

'Now my heart is troubled, and what shall I say? "Father, save me from this hour"? No, it was for this very reason I came to this hour. Father, glorify your name!'

Then a voice came from heaven, 'I have glorified it, and will glorify it again' (John 12:23, 27–8).

'Father, the time has come. Glorify your Son, that your Son may glorify you . . . I have brought you glory on earth by completing the work you gave me to do. And now, Father, glorify me in your presence with the glory I had with you before the world began' (John 17:1, 4–5).

There on the Cross, Jesus revealed to all, for all time, God's repugnance for sin and His unutterable love for the sinner. And if we are to reveal God in all His beauty and glory to the world in which we live today, we will have to be purged of all that is not holy – for God's holiness and His glory walk hand-in-hand. As our faith is tried, like gold in the fire, Jesus will be glorified. His face and character will shine through us as all impurities are purged out of us:

> These have come so that your faith – of greater worth than gold, which perishes even though refined by fire – may be proved genuine and may result in praise, glory and honour when Jesus Christ is revealed. Though you have not seen him, you love him; and even though you do not see him now, you believe in him and are filled with an inexpressible and glorious joy (1 Pet. 1:7–8).

We are told to so live that others, seeing our good works, will glorify our Father in heaven (Matt. 5:16). Daily living to the glory of God will include suffering for all of us, one way or another. Jesus said to His disciples:

> No-one who has left home or brothers or sisters or mother or father or children or fields for me and the gospel will fail to receive a hundred times as much in this present age (homes, brothers, sisters, mothers, children and fields – and with them persecutions) and in the age to come, eternal life (Mark 10:29–30).

If I want to be with Jesus in His glory, and if I want to share in His eternal inheritance in heaven, then I must be willing to suffer with Him whilst here on earth. He clearly told us, through His disciple Peter:

> Dear friends, do not be surprised at the painful trial you are suffering, as though something

strange were happening to you. But rejoice that
you participate in the sufferings of Christ, so that
you may be overjoyed when his glory is revealed
(1 Pet. 4:12–13).

and also:

The God of all grace, who called you to his
eternal glory in Christ, after you have suffered
a little while, will himself restore you and make
you strong, firm and steadfast (1 Pet. 5:10).

The Fellowship of his Sufferings

A hillside garden near a city gate,
    And One alone under the olive trees,
And one outside irresolute, who late
    Has lingered, and did now himself bewail,
    'I pray Thee let the cup pass, for I fail
    Before such agony, I cannot drink,
    Save me, O Lord, I sink! –
Confounded by this anguish, my heart sees
Only a horror of great darkness wait
        Under the olive trees.'

'I wait.' The little leaves moved at the word,
    A cloud obscured the bright face of the moon.
The lover listened, something in him stirred –
    'Did ever Lover thus entreat before?
    I may not call me lover any more,
    For never love grieved Love as I have grieved,
    And yet I had believed
    Myself Thy lover; soon, Beloved, soon
Thou wilt be far from me; for I have heard
    And disobeyed Thee.'

        But the Paschal moon
Sudden shone out, flooding the darkened air,
    And all the open space between the trees;
The very garden seemed as if aware

Of holy presences. Then to that place
Ran in the lover, fell upon his face;
    No word he spoke; no chiding word was spoken;
    But as one smitten, broken,
As one who cannot comfort or appease
Accusing conscience, dumb he waited there,
    Under the olive trees.

*   *   *   *   *   *   *   *   *   *

The night dews rose, and all the garden wept,
    As if it could not ever smile again;
The night wind woke and mourned with him, and swept
            and swept
    The hillside sadly; and as in a glass,
    Darkly distinct, he saw a vision pass
        Of One who took the cup, alone, alone,
        Then broke from Him a moan,
A cry to God for pain, for any pain
Save this last desolation; and he crept
    In penitence to his Lord's feet again.

Then all the garden held its breath for awe;
    A lighted silence hung among the trees;
The blessed angels, glad because the law,
    Love's law, had wooed him,
            waiting near heard speech
    Not to be uttered, spiritual, out of reach,
        Of earthly language. Low the lover lay
        Adoring Him whose way
Is to enrich with such sweet mysteries.
Never an angel told the things he saw
    Under the olive trees.

Never an angel told, but this I know,
    That he to whom that night Gethsemane
Opened its secrets, cannot help but go
    Softly thereafter, as one lately shriven,
    Passionately loving, as one much forgiven.
        And never, never can his heart forget

That Head with hair all wet
  With the red dews of Love's extremity,
Those eyes from which fountains of love did flow,
  There in the Garden of Gethsemane.

Amy Carmichael, 'Toward Jerusalem'

How do we share in His sufferings?

When we speak, as Paul did when he wrote to the Philippians from a Roman prison cell, of *the fellowship of Christ's sufferings*, we speak of 'The Cup'. This is very holy ground, and we need to tread very gently. One thing is certain, God does not force this fellowship on us. He invites us to join Him: He seeks for our voluntary cooperation. When I give Him my will and let go of my supposed rights to my own choices, then I am ready for God to put His yoke on my neck; I am ready for Him to wrap the towel around me for His service; and I am making myself ready for Him to offer me His cup.

At the beginning of this chapter, we read about the disciples' conversation in Mark 10. They were discussing among themselves as to who would be the greatest in the Kingdom of Heaven. Each one of them wanted to be the VIP – it wasn't just James and John who had this ambition, though they voiced the question: it was all of them! That's why the others were so angry, the two had forestalled them, getting in with their request before they had a chance. Each one wanted to be a big white chief, to be a colonel in God's army – none was willing to be a non-commissioned officer, let alone an ordinary soldier.

Jesus didn't argue with them, but He explained how to become great in His Kingdom. In a catchy slogan, He might have said, 'The way to *up* is *down*.'

'Can you drink the *cup* . . . ?' He asked them.

The cup may be full of joy, so that one is deeply conscious that one's lines have been cast in pleasant places: but, much more likely, it may be filled with suffering, heartache, burdens almost too great to bear.

Pause again and think of our Lord in the Garden and that heartbreaking request that was wrung from Him, 'Let this cup pass from me!'

Without question, the depths of His suffering on the Cross of Calvary, as He became our sin and died a death to expiate that sin, cannot be tasted by another. We can never enter into that; nor will we ever know the anguish of that bitter cry: 'My God, my God, why have you forsaken me?' But, nevertheless, we are invited to share with Christ in His sufferings. The disciples simply did not understand what Christ was asking of them, 'You don't know what you are asking,' Jesus said. 'Can you drink the cup I drink or be baptised with the baptism I am baptised with?' (Mark 10:38) and they unhesitatingly said: Yes!

'You shall indeed,' Jesus replied, and though they did not then understand what would be involved, in the years that lay ahead they did enter into those sufferings. James was killed by Herod and John was exiled on Patmos by the Roman provincial governors – but they didn't understand Christ's words at the time that they were uttered.

It was as though Christ said to them, 'You shall indeed drink of My cup, and then you will learn that the way to greatness is by suffering – through the bitter to the sweet, through the cup to the fellowship.'

With their human limitations hemming in their understanding and the worldly examples on all sides pointing to a reverse solution to their quest, the Lord went on to show them, as clearly as He could, that if you want to be chief you have to learn to become servant of all.

> Jesus called them [His twelve disciples] together and said, 'You know that those who are regarded as rulers of the Gentiles lord it over them, and their high officials exercise authority over them. Not so with you. Instead, whoever wants to become great among you must be your servant, and whoever wants to be first must be slave of all' (Mark 10:42–4).

Jesus had given them an example of true godly greatness when He, the suffering Servant of Isaiah's prophecy, washed their feet, making Himself of no greater importance than the lowest slave. 'For even the Son of Man did not come to be served, but to serve, and to give his life as a ransom for many' (Mark 10:45).

Christ was crucified to redeem us. Could He go any lower? He died to save the lowest, meanest, worst criminal as well as the most respectable, upright, clean-living sinner. He died in order to become our sin; to accept our deserved wages; to pay the price of our ransom, our redemption. What more could He have given? How much lower could He have stooped? *And yet* . . . He was Almighty God! He is the King of kings and the Lord of lords. He was not demeaned by becoming servant of all, by stooping so low to serve us. Not a bit of it! He was very God of very God, eternally equal to Father and Spirit, our Saviour:

. . . perfect through suffering (Heb. 2:10).

. . . and, once made perfect, he became the source of eternal salvation for all who obey him (Heb. 5:9).

. . . we see Jesus . . . now crowned with glory and honour (Heb. 2:9).

> Therefore God exalted him to the
> highest place
> and gave him the name that is above
> every name.

(Phil. 2:9)

Our nearness to our Lord will be measured, not by our capacity for joy, but by our capacity for suffering. When we suffer with Jesus and for Jesus, we enter into the truest possible fellowship with Him. When we *choose* to bear the cross – remember, we don't *have* to – we shall drink from that cup and we shall enter that fellowship.

Let us look briefly at four specific ways in which Christ suffers as He looks at our world, and then we will look at three specific ways in which we can seek to share in those sufferings with Him.

Firstly, there is a deep spiritual level of suffering that comes from a burden for the lost and a true passion for the souls of men. Christ knew that the lost were lost. It makes a mockery of the Cross if they are not. To believe that the lost are not lost makes us judges of God Himself. How could God send His only begotten Son to that cruel death of crucifixion at the hands of brutal soldiers, if they were not lost and if all humankind could be saved by any other means? No, God's holy laws declare that the lost are lost, however we choose to define the word and describe the state. People without Christ are without hope, and will spend all eternity in the absence of His presence. By rejecting Him, they have chosen their lot. It is not God who condemns them, but they are condemned by their own choice to remain lost.

There are some three thousand million people alive in our world today who have had no human chance to turn to and accept Christ as their personal Saviour. Do our hearts break at that thought? Do we feel guilty that we do so little about it; that we care so little; that this fact does not give us sleepless nights? Have we a burden for the lost?

That burden tires the body, wears it out, drives it to its utmost limit as it seeks ways of serving and of taking Christ to the masses. Jesus knew that physical weariness and fatigue.

People sometimes say to missionaries (and others in Christian service, I have no doubt), 'You mustn't burn the candle at both ends or you will wear yourself out' ... or to use a more up-to-date phrase, 'Be careful or you'll suffer burn-out!' Why shouldn't we suffer burn-out? Why do I need to be careful to preserve my body, mind and soul from physical fatigue? Why do I need to demand my right to holidays and reasonable (by our human reckoning) breaks? If I die, I'm going to be with Christ for ever; if the lost die, they are going to be without Him for ever. Must I not seek every means to reach them 'as long as it is day . . . night is coming, when no-one can work' (John 9:4) – even if I upset the chemical balance of my body for a short spell? *Jesus Christ suffers for the lost.*

Secondly, there is a suffering of spirit that comes from being in the presence of sin. It is all too easy for us to come to terms with sin. We hear so much bad language, blasphemy, using of the Lord's name in vain, that it is possible to cease to notice it, so that it no longer hurts us. A few years ago a Christian would have refused to listen to – indeed, turned off – certain radio and/or television programmes, because of the free use of words that we would not use ourselves and the portrayal of acts of violence or sexual permissiveness. In fact, many would have made the effort to write to the controllers and lodge a complaint at the use of a public facility in a way obnoxious to the Christian conscience. Today, we hear and see so much that is unwholesome and ungodly that we may have become inured to it, and find ourselves listening or watching with hardly a flicker of doubt as to the propriety of doing so.

Sin crucified our Lord Jesus Christ: despite the savage cruelty of the nails, our sin crushed His Spirit even more deeply than the nails His body. Does sin still affect me like that? Do I long to be delivered from the filth and horror of sin that I see all around me? Am I prepared to stand up and be counted? Do I speak up when I hear swearing and obscenities, asking the perpetrator to stop? Or am I too fearful to take any sort of action? Or does it just no longer hurt me, because I have become too accustomed to it to notice it? If we are yoked to Jesus Christ, we shall *suffer*, as He does, *in the presence of sin.*

Thirdly, Christ suffered with the sufferings and needs of others. He took all the sufferings of mankind into His great heart, and ached for the sufferers. He felt their pain. When the widow lady walked slowly, with down-bent head, beside the coffin of her only son, her heart breaking with unspoken grief, Jesus became conscious of her; He left the crowd around Him, crossed over to her, and shared in her grief momentarily before He raised her son to life again. When mothers pressed upon Him with their children, though He had had a busy day of ministry, He had compassion on them and made them feel welcome, and blessed their children. When He was faced by the woman taken in adultery, He felt her pain and shame, and so caused the watching, critical crowd to depart before He spoke to her. Always, always, He felt the heartbeat of the other one and met them at the point of their need.

Do we get so accustomed to seeing suffering – the terrible unbelievable plight of refugees, with neither food nor clothing, on a barren snow-clad mountainside; flies crawling over the eyes of starving African children; whole villages washed away in a tidal wave of destruction in some monsoon-struck country; thousands made homeless in an earthquake in Russia or South America – that we can no longer react? Have our hearts become hardened, in order to protect ourselves from this avalanche of suffering? Do I just feel that I cannot go on feeling for others: I am drained and exhausted by it? Do I sense that there is just too much suffering in the world for any one heart to carry it all?

Or am I still longing for Jesus to make me and keep me sensitive to the needs of others, at whatever cost to myself? Oh, that I may never cease to be willing to *suffer for the needs of others* – let me drink this cup with Jesus.

Fourthly, does not Christ suffer because of the terrible apathy of His own family to do anything to help those millions in their need? I recently read the diary of James Gilmour of Mongolia, who was known as the pioneer of blood. Living in great privation and poverty, in a harsh inclement climate, often without even the bare necessities of life, he saw his dear wife die under the suffering that such living caused them. Eventually, he gave his own life for those rugged people – all because of a passionate love for them and a frantic desire that, at any cost, they should come to hear of and turn to the Saviour. At the end of his life, one of the last entries in his diary was: 'In the shape of converts, I have seen no results. Not even one wants to be a Christian!' Can you sense the deep poignancy and pathos behind those words – the burning ache in his heart for those who have spurned his Saviour, despite his every endeavour?

'O Jerusalem, Jerusalem,' our Lord cried, 'how often I have longed to gather your children together . . . but you were not willing!' (Luke 13:34). Was it not a cry of heart bitterness, wrung from the Master, because of their apathy and indifference? Yes, indeed, Jesus *suffers because of the apathy* of those who should know better.

How can we enter in, to share in the fellowship of His sufferings? Perhaps we can touch on three basic principles that the Bible reveals to us, by which we can make such fellowship a reality in our lives.

i) Through thanksgiving in all things

He took the *cup*, gave thanks and offered it to them (Matt. 26:27).

A different cup, you want to suggest? But no! This cup is mentioned within the context of those last two days of His earthly life. On the way to Jerusalem, He asked them as they were arguing as to who should be the greatest, 'Can you drink the cup I drink?' (Mark 10:38) Then, in the Upper Room, 'He took the cup, gave thanks . . . ' (Matt. 26:27). Only an hour or so later, after they had sung a hymn and gone out to the Garden of Gethsemane, He distanced Himself from His disciples, threw Himself down on the ground and poured out His heart to His Father, 'O Father, if it is possible, may this cup be taken from me!' (Matt. 26:39)

Could these three really be different cups? In the heart and mind of Christ, surely it was one and the same cup in each of those three incidents.

Paul wrote to the Philippians from his prison cell in Rome, 'Do not be anxious about anything, but in everything by prayer and petition, with thanksgiving, present your requests to God' (Phil. 4:6).

Would you bear with me if I seek to share with you, once again, one of the deepest moments in my own spiritual pilgrimage, when He taught me this truth, perhaps from a slightly different angle than I had previously seen it? It occurred in the middle of a night of physical violence and brutality. Taken by a group of savage guerrilla soldiers during the civil war of the sixties in the ex-Belgian Congo, I had been beaten up, threatened, kicked . . . and I felt terribly alone. Just for a moment, God seemed very far away – almost remote. Could He not have stepped in and protected me? Didn't He care?

Driven down the short corridor of my home, almost sick with fear and apprehension, I suddenly knew that God was speaking to me and, in a strangely wonderful way, a great peace took possession of my tortured mind. Later on, looking back on that night and seeking to know what it was that He had said to me, I became conscious of this simple question, 'Can you thank Me for trusting you with this experience, even if I never tell you why?'

He did not ask me to thank Him for the savage cruelty, no, but for showing His trust in me. That is an amazing thought. I know that we trust Him, but it was a new thought that He wanted to be able to trust me. 'Yes,' He seemed to say, 'of course I could have prevented this happening. I could have taken you out of this situation. But it would help Me, in My bigger plan for others, if you could accept to go through this with Me, without turning on Me or accusing Me of deserting you, or even asking Me for a detailed explanation.'

It was awesomely humbling, to think that God had been willing to trust me with some part of the fulfilment

of a plan of His, even if it was beyond my present understanding. 'Can you thank Me . . . ?' Yes, by His grace I
could and, as I did so, peace flowed into my innermost
being. This did not stop or even lessen the pain and
cruelty, but suddenly, it made everything different – I
was now suffering with Christ, in Christ, for Christ – the
whole experience became a privilege! And the entry to
that sense of privilege was thanksgiving. For me, that
night became a tiny sip of His cup.

ii) Through self-denial at all times

'Father,' he [Jesus] said, 'everything is possible for you.
Take this cup from me. Yet not what I will, but what
you will' (Mark 14:36).

Surely our Lord and Master exercised the most amazing self-denial at the most crucial moment of His life!
No one would have blamed Him if He had called upon
His Father to send those legions of angels that always
stand ready to obey His slightest command, to take
Him out of this world, back into glory. There was the
human cry of fear: He knew His Father could do it!
'Take this cup from me,' – but by a superhuman effort,
strengthened by angels, out of a lifetime's practice of
obedience to His Father, He added: 'Yet not what I will,
but what you will.' He denied His right to receive power
from on high to avoid the Cross.

In the same way, as He hung on the Cross, and those
who passed by hurled insults at Him, 'So! You who are
going to destroy the temple and build it in three days,
come down from the cross and save yourself!' (Mark
15:29–30)

He exercised supreme self-denial, and answered them
not a word. In the same way the chief priests and the
teachers of the law mocked Him, 'He saved others,' they
said, 'but he can't save himself! Let this Christ, this King
of Israel, come down now from the cross, that we may
see and believe' (Mark 15:31–2).

Again He denied His right to receive power from on high to come down from the Cross. Had He saved Himself, He could never have saved us. Though they might have seen Him, had He come down from the Cross, there would have been nothing left in which they could have believed.

Oh, how deeply Christ understands that to which He calls us, when He tells us to deny ourselves! 'If anyone would come after me, he must deny himself and take up his cross daily and follow me' (Luke 9:23). And where was He going at the moment when He said those words and invited us to follow Him? Had He not set His face to go up to Jerusalem, where Elders, Scribes and Pharisees were waiting to hand Him over to Pilate and the Roman authorities, that they might crucify Him? His invitation is to deny ourselves and our 'rights' to live, and to follow Him to crucifixion, to a total death of self that others may live.

Can I grasp that? To deny myself is contrary to all normally acceptable teaching in the world around me. Everyone else seeks to assert their own moral worth: to come to terms with their self-image and then to set about improving it. The whole ethos of today is self-assertion, each one standing up for his or her rights – 'Haven't I a right to be considered?' and such-like aspirations. We are repeatedly assured that we mustn't allow ourselves to be trampled on, ignored, taken for granted, manipulated. Yet, if I deny myself and agree with God that I have no rights – that all He gives me is by grace, and not by merit – I may well be trampled on, ignored, taken for granted and even manipulated by the world around me. This certainly is not the route for worldly promotion!

When a situation has developed in which there has perhaps been a gross injustice, a libel, or false accusation – and I long to cry out for vindication, 'Haven't I at least the right to clear my name?' – can I instead take my hands off the proceedings and trust the whole thing to God, saying, 'Not my will, but Yours be done'? That will be a sip from His cup. Hasn't the Holy Spirit told us:

Christ suffered for you,
leaving you an example . . .
He committed no sin, and no deceit was found in
his mouth:
when they hurled their insults at him, he did not
retaliate;
when he suffered, he made no threats.
Instead he entrusted himself to him who judges
justly.

(1 Peter 2:21–3)

We too can commit ourselves and our cause to Him who
judges righteously and knows all the truth, and needs
not for us to vindicate ourselves.

iii) Through identification with all people

Christ wept over Jerusalem; He wept at the grave of
Lazarus.

Paul certainly knew how to be identified with all
people: 'I have become all things to all men so that
by all possible means I might save some' (1 Cor. 9:22).
Later, in his second recorded letter to the Corinthians,
he lists some of what he suffered, comparing himself
with those who avoided all such sufferings:

I have worked much harder, been in prison more
frequently, been flogged more severely, and been
exposed to death again and again. Five times I
received from the Jews the forty lashes minus
one. Three times I was beaten with rods, once
I was stoned, three times I was shipwrecked, I
spent a night and a day in the open sea, I have
been constantly on the move. I have been in danger
from rivers, in danger from bandits, in danger from
my own countrymen, in danger from Gentiles; in
danger in the city, in danger in the country, in
danger at sea; and in danger from false brothers.

I have laboured and toiled and have often gone
without sleep; I have known hunger and thirst and
have often gone without food; I have been cold and
naked. Besides everything else, I face daily the
pressure of my concern for all the churches. Who
is weak, and I do not feel weak? Who is led into
sin, and I do not inwardly burn? (2 Cor. 11:23–9).

Do we weep with those who weep as well as rejoice with
those who rejoice? Are we willing to become deeply
involved in the pains and sufferings of others even if
this intrudes into our private lives, even if this prevents
us from having time to ourselves or any privacy? Thus
can we sip His cup. Thus was He involved for us.

I wonder if any of my readers has read or heard the
prayer of Lady Julian of Norwich, written 600 years
ago, during the fourteenth century:

I conceived a great desire, and prayed our Lord
God that He would grant me in the course of
my life three wounds, that is:

– the wound of contrition;
– the wound of compassion;
– the wound of longing with my will for God.

This I asked without condition. Amen.

Dare we enter into the spirit of that prayer as we seek
to know something of the fellowship of our Saviour's
sufferings?

O God, please give me three wounds:

– the wound of contrition, firstly for my own
sins of disobedience, of commission and also of
omission, and then for the sins of the world; and
with this wounding, that You would place upon

me Your yoke, granting me the grace of submission
to Your perfect will;

– the wound of compassion for my fellow-men,
seeing them as those in need of Your love rather
than my criticism; in need of Your humble service
rather than my proud aloofness; and with this
wounding, that You would gird me with Your
towel, and fill me with Your humility to serve
others as You have served me;

– the wound of longing with my will for God and
Your holiness, of hungering and thirsting after
righteousness, of seeking by all means to be available to watch with You one hour wheresoever
You invite me; and with this wounding, that You
would present me with Your cup, and the infinite and inestimable privilege of sharing in the
fellowship of Your suffering.

And all this I ask, without condition. Amen.

Dare I pray such a prayer? Dare I actually *seek wounds*
from the tender hand of God as His free gift to me? Lady
Julian asked for all this, only and solely for God's glory,
and not her own. It was utterly unselfish. There was no
hidden motive or concealed desire for personal gain.
Do I weep for my sins, and then identify myself with
the sins of the world and weep again – as Daniel did?
Do I weep over the lost, and agonise to find ways of
involvement in God's programme to reach them with
the Gospel? Can I cry out, 'Oh, God, that I might want
You so badly that it becomes a wound in my heart!' 'As
the deer pants for streams of water,' wrote the Psalmist,
'so my soul pants for you, O God!' (Ps. 42:1).
    Maybe I would be forgiven for re-writing Paul's prayer
as follows:

I want to know Christ – and to be yoked to Him

so that I can learn of Him and become meek and lowly as He is;

and the power of His resurrection – which alone will enable me to be small enough in my own eyes that I may be girded with the towel to serve others with His own humility;

and the fellowship of sharing in His sufferings – partaking with Him of His cup, as I seek to know something of suffering as He suffered on behalf of others;

becoming like Him in His death. Amen.

(Phil. 3:10)

Epilogue

The Peace of True Fellowship in the Church

The triangle is complete: each angle and each side equal and bound together with a strength that emanates from the omnipotent God.

In seeking to understand the innermost meaning of the word *koinonia*, we have seen that our most basic need is to have a living, vital relationship with God, as children with their Father, and this is made possible to us through the sacrifice of God's Son, the Lord Jesus Christ, on the Cross of Calvary. This relationship is worked out in practical details in our daily lives as we submit ourselves voluntarily to God's authority, being yoked to Him and walking in step beside Him.

Secondly, we have seen that God wants us to enjoy *koinonia* with our fellow-men. As we seek to relate to them with a Christ-like humility, we shall reveal that relationship by actively serving them. We shall be willing for God to gird us with the towel, and to make us conscious of how He wants us to serve. When we accept this as God's will for all His children, then we can see that in fact it is not so much *us* serving them, but God Himself serving them through us.

Thirdly, we have sought to understand something of the suffering of God for all the world. In amazing condescension, He stoops to invite us to allow ourselves to be drawn up, as it were, from our corner of the triangle (where we allowed Him to suffer for others through us), into the third side of it, thus giving us the privilege of sharing directly in the fellowship of His own sufferings. As we seek to enter into this, we shall at least sip from the cup that He drank for us.

The *yoke*, that binds each one of us individually to Almighty God, is a symbol of submissive obedience, and thus reminds us of our need for the sacrifice (if we can call it such) of our self-sufficiency. As we pause to think about it, we can see that the yoke conceals a paradox, that in submission to Christ we can find our greatest freedom.

Submission and yoking sound like words of subservience and imprisonment. But as we agree to hand over control of our lives to Christ, voluntarily and willingly, we find not only that we have a new Master, but also that He is a wondrously kind and amazingly trusting Master. He imparts to us not only the ability to do the task to which He calls us, but He also provides all the strength needed. He takes far more than half the load! Instead of now having to carry responsibility for all decisions and then being imprisoned by the consequences, we find that as He makes the decisions and we bow to obey, we are wonderfully free to enjoy the outcome. We have indeed become 'partakers of the divine nature' (2 Pet. 1:4, AV) – this is at the very heart of *koinonia*.

The *towel*, with which God wishes to gird us so that we can serve one another, is a symbol of humility, and so reminds us that there is no room for pride in the life of a Christian. If we stop to consider it, the towel reveals the paradox that in service *for* Christ, we can exercise the greatest authority.

Towels and basins and dirty feet, including stooping down before our fellow-men sounds again like subservience and being the underdog – it certainly does not bear the connotation of having authority! And yet, as we submit to God's direction and allow Him to gird us, in spirit and mind as well as body, to serve others as He served us, we find that, even though we may be trampled upon, left while others are promoted, or even relegated to the lower echelons of society as far as humanity is concerned, our spirits are suddenly liberated from the drive and tension of all around us. We are freed to be ourselves, at rest in God, with His peace filling our souls. Once the pressure – to be a success, to make money, to get on in the world, to be seen to be somebody – has been removed, we are free to be ourselves, and as such we have spiritual authority in the realm of prayer and of compassion and of mature judgment. We have indeed become 'partakers of the heavenly calling' (Heb. 3:1, AV), which is true *koinonia*, fellowship with God the Father, God the Son and God the Holy Spirit, as well as fellowship with our fellow-men.

The *cup* that God drank to the dregs, that He might save humankind, is a symbol of fellowship *and* suffering. As we contemplate the invitation to share it with our Lord and Saviour we know that, should we accept the privilege, we will have to give up all rights to self-determination and to our natural inclination to avoid suffering. The cup also offers us a paradox, that in suffering *with* Christ, we are perfected for glory.

To drink a cup of bitterness – with a life possibly made up of intense loneliness; a willingness to be abused without retaliating or hitting back or seeking to justify oneself; of being grossly misunderstood, falsely accused, considered contemptible, despised and rejected; of betrayal, desertion, with mental and/or physical torture – this hardly sounds like a recipe for glory! And yet, when all such is borne 'for the sake of the Name of Christ', He tells us we are to consider ourselves blessed. 'But even if you should suffer for what is right, you are blessed,' Peter tells us, adding the wonderful explanation for such a strange statement:

> For Christ died for sins . . . do not be surprised at the painful trial you are suffering, as though something strange were happening to you. But rejoice that you participate in the sufferings of Christ, so that you may be overjoyed when his glory is revealed. If you are insulted because of the name of Christ, you are blessed, for the Spirit of glory and of God rests on you (1 Pet. 3:14,18 and 4:12–14).

Paul, after a life of untold hardship and suffering as a pioneer missionary, wrote, 'For our light and momentary troubles are achieving for us an eternal glory that far outweighs them all' (2 Cor. 4:17). To be allowed the privilege of being a 'partaker' of Christ's sufferings' (1 Pet. 4:13, AV) is the final wonder of true *koinonia*.

As the three sides of our triangle meet and form a meaningful whole, we can now know with utmost certainty of spirit that we are 'complete in him, which is the head of all principality and power' (Col. 2:10, AV). 'Make every effort to be found spotless, blameless and at peace with him' (2 Pet. 3:14).

If we are complete in Him, the outstanding witness to this completeness will be His *peace* abiding in our hearts. He promised to give us His *peace* (John 14:27); He promised to fill us with His *joy* (John 15:11); and the context of both these promises is His *love*:

As the Father has loved me, so have I loved you
... My command is this: Love each other as I have
loved you. Greater love has no-one than this, that
he lay down his life for his friends (John 15:9,
12–13).

Love, joy, peace – the fruit of the Spirit, which results
as we are 'made partakers of the Holy Ghost' (Heb. 6:4,
AV); so we enjoy complete *koinonia* with the Godhead
and with our neighbours.

> As for God, his way is perfect ...
> It is God who arms me with strength,
>   and makes my way perfect.

(Ps. 18:30,32)

May we be found perfectly willing to enter into the
fullness of a living fellowship with God and our fellow-
men, on God's terms, however contrary these may
seem to man's natural inclinations and so-called logical
thinking.

We proclaim to you what we have seen and heard,
so that you also may have fellowship with us. And
our fellowship is with the Father and with his
Son, Jesus Christ. We write this to make our joy
complete.
This is the message we have heard from him
and declare to you: God is light; in him there is
no darkness at all. If we claim to have fellowship
with him yet walk in the darkness, we lie and do
not live by the truth. But if we walk in the light,
as he is in the light, we have fellowship with one
another, and the blood of Jesus, his Son, purifies
us from all sin (1 John 1:3–7).